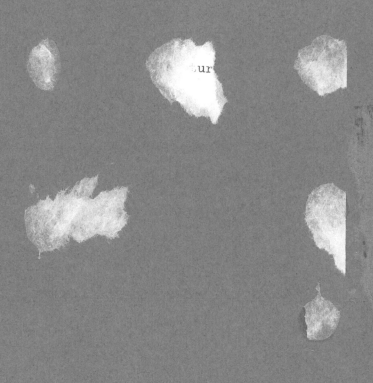

1900
Volume I 1910

*Other Publications:*
UNDERSTANDING COMPUTERS
YOUR HOME
THE ENCHANTED WORLD
THE KODAK LIBRARY OF CREATIVE PHOTOGRAPHY
GREAT MEALS IN MINUTES
THE CIVIL WAR
PLANET EARTH
COLLECTOR'S LIBRARY OF THE CIVIL WAR
THE EPIC OF FLIGHT
THE GOOD COOK
THE SEAFARERS
WORLD WAR II
HOME REPAIR AND IMPROVEMENT
THE OLD WEST

For information on and a full description of any of the Time-Life Books series listed above, please write:
Reader Information
Time-Life Books
641 North Fairbanks Court
Chicago, Illinois 60611

This volume is one of a series
that chronicles American culture from 1870 to 1970.

# This Fabulous Century

Volume I

# 1900 1910

By the Editors of TIME-LIFE BOOKS

862114

Time-Life Books, Alexandria, Virginia

Time-Life Books Inc.
is a wholly owned subsidiary of

# TIME INCORPORATED

FOUNDER: Henry R. Luce 1898-1967

*Editor-in-Chief:* Henry Anatole Grunwald
*President:* J. Richard Munro
*Chairman of the Board:* Ralph P. Davidson
*Corporate Editor:* Jason McManus
*Group Vice President, Books:* Reginald K. Brack Jr.
*Vice President, Books:* George Artandi

## TIME-LIFE BOOKS INC.

EDITOR: George Constable
*Executive Editor:* George Daniels
*Editorial General Manager:* Neal Goff
*Director of Design:* Louis Klein
*Editorial Board:* Dale M. Brown, Roberta Conlan,
Ellen Phillips, Gerry Schremp, Gerald Simons,
Rosalind Stubenberg, Kit van Tulleken, Henry Woodhead
*Director of Research:* Phyllis K. Wise
*Director of Photography:* John Conrad Weiser

PRESIDENT: William J. Henry
*Senior Vice President:* Christopher T. Linen
*Vice Presidents:* Stephen L. Bair, Robert A. Ellis,
John M. Fahey Jr., Juanita T. James, James L. Mercer,
Joanne A. Pello, Paul R. Stewart, Christian Strasser

## THIS FABULOUS CENTURY

EDITOR: Ezra Bowen
Editorial Staff for *Volume I, 1900-1910*
*Picture Editor:* Mary Y. Steinbauer
*Designer:* John R. Martinez
*Staff Writers:* George Constable,
Anne Horan, Bryce S. Walker
*Researchers:* Alice Baker, Nancy Cabasin,
Terry Drucker, Helen Greenway, Helen Lapham,
Victoria Winterer, Linda Wolfe
*Copy Coordinator:* Susan B. Galloway
*Picture Coordinator:* Barbara S. Simon

EDITORIAL OPERATIONS
*Design:* Ellen Robling (assistant director)
*Copy Room:* Diane Ullius
*Editorial Operations:* Caroline A. Boubin (manager)
*Production:* Celia Beattie
*Quality Control:* James J. Cox (director), Sally Collins
*Library:* Louise D. Forstall

*Correspondents:* Elisabeth Kraemer-Singh (Bonn); Margot Hapgood, Dorothy Bacon (London); Miriam Hsia, Susan Jonas, Lucy T. Voulgaris (New York); Maria Vincenza Aloisi, Josephine du Brusle (Paris); Ann Natanson (Rome). Valuable assistance was also provided by: Reg Murphy (Atlanta); Sue Wymelenberg (Boston); Robert Buyer (Buffalo); Richard Rawe (Cincinnati); Richard Wooten (Cleveland); Holland McCombs (Dallas); Blanche Hardin (Denver); Julie Greenwalt (Detroit); Gayle Rosenberg (Los Angeles); Don Davies (Madison); Jane Rieker (Miami); Rod Van Every (Milwaukee); Patricia Chander (New Orleans); Carolyn T. Chubet (New York); Sandra Hinson (Orlando); Jane Beatty (Philadelphia); Sherley Uhl (Pittsburgh); Martha Green (San Francisco); Jane Estes (Seattle); Frank Leeming Jr. (St. Louis); Lucille Larkin (Washington, D.C.).

**PRINTED IN JAPAN**

# Contents

# Introduction

*At the outgoing of the old and the incoming of the new century you begin the last session of the Fifty-sixth Congress with evidences on every hand of individual and national prosperity and with proof of the growing strength and increasing power for good of Republican institutions.*

PRESIDENT WILLIAM McKINLEY TO THE CONGRESS, DECEMBER 3, 1900

When President McKinley proudly addressed the Congress at the turn of the century, America was a country very different from the colossus it was to become. The statistics of the period (imperfect though they were in those non-computerized times) illustrate the contrast dramatically. In 1900 there were only 45 states—despite the optimistic 48-star flag on page 19. The total U.S. population was 76,094,000—barely two fifths what it would be six decades later. The average American worker earned 22¢ an hour. Automobiles were selling for about $1,550 each; and the truck and bus were still to be invented. In any case, fewer than 150 miles of paved highway existed in the whole United States.

Keeping up with the Joneses had not yet become a national religion. Only about 18 people in every 1,000 owned a telephone, and there was still no such thing as a radio or an electric ice box or most of the other symbols of modern domestic consumership. People had other, more fundamental things to worry about. Diphtheria, typhoid and malaria were among the leading causes of death. A cold might easily develop into pneumonia, and more often than not, pneumonia was fatal.

The most crowded occupation in the United States in 1900 was agriculture, for nearly 11 million people were farmers. But times were changing. Factory employment was already over six million and climbing fast. Nearly half a million immigrants poured into the country in 1900; within five years the annual total would be over a million. These newcomers were bringing change with them, and by their ways and their sheer numbers, too, they would help to cause change.

But in 1900, most of the changes had not yet taken hold. Life across the predominantly rural countryside was still relatively simple and, as President McKinley noted in his Congressional message, quite good. For almost two full generations there had been no major wars. This, too, seemed quite proper. The business of America was peace—peace and prosperity. And it was a fact that in this simple time even the U.S. Government was prosperous: in 1900 the Treasury showed a surplus of $46,380,000 in income over expenditures. This happy circumstance would occur again from time to time until 1960 *(page 9)* when President Dwight D. Eisenhower proudly balanced the U.S. national budget for the last time—while standing in a hole of gross debt so deep that the achievement was barely visible.

| Rank | | 1900 | 1960 | Rank |
|---|---|---|---|---|
| 31 | Colorado | 539,700 | 1,753,947 | 33 |
| 32 | Florida | 528,542 | 4,951,560 | 10 |
| 33 | Washington | 518,103 | 2,853,214 | 23 |
| 34 | Rhode Island | 428,556 | 859,488 | 39 |
| 35 | Oregon | 413,536 | 1,768,687 | 32 |
| 36 | New Hampshire | 411,588 | 606,921 | 46 |
| 37 | South Dakota | 401,570 | 680,514 | 41 |
| 38 | *Oklahoma Terr. | 398,331 | 2,328,284 | 27 |
| 39 | *Indian Terr. | 392,060 | | |
| 40 | Vermont | 343,641 | 389,881 | 48 |
| 41 | North Dakota | 319,146 | 632,446 | 45 |
| 42 | Dist. of Columbia | 278,718 | 763,956 | 40 |
| 43 | Utah | 276,749 | 890,627 | 38 |
| 44 | Montana | 243,329 | 674,767 | 42 |
| 45 | **New Mexico Terr. | 195,310 | 951,023 | 37 |
| 46 | Delaware | 184,735 | 446,292 | 47 |
| 47 | Idaho | 161,772 | 667,191 | 43 |
| 48 | **Hawaii Terr. | 154,001 | 632,772 | 44 |
| 49 | **Arizona Terr. | 122,931 | 1,302,161 | 35 |
| 50 | Wyoming | 92,531 | 330,066 | 49 |
| 51 | **Alaska Terr. | 63,592 | 226,167 | 51 |
| 52 | Nevada | 42,335 | 285,278 | 50 |

*Joined to become Oklahoma state 1907   **Became state after 1910*

## Population

| | 1900 | 1960 |
|---|---|---|
| TOTAL UNITED STATES | 76,094,000 | 179,323,000 |
| URBAN (2500 or more) | 30,160,000 | 113,056,000 |
| Per cent | 40% | 63% |
| RURAL | 45,835,000 | 66,267,000 |
| Per cent | 60% | 37% |
| | | |
| Native born white | 56,595,000 | 149,544,000 |
| Foreign born white | 10,214,000 | 9,294,000 |
| Negro | 8,834,000 | 18,849,000 |
| American Indian | 237,000 | 547,000 |
| Oriental | 114,000 | 709,000 |

### STATES BY POPULATION

| Rank | | 1900 | 1960 | Rank |
|---|---|---|---|---|
| 1 | New York | 7,268,894 | 16,782,304 | 1 |
| 2 | Pennsylvania | 6,302,115 | 11,319,366 | 3 |
| 3 | Illinois | 4,821,550 | 10,081,158 | 4 |
| 4 | Ohio | 4,157,545 | 9,706,397 | 5 |
| 5 | Missouri | 3,106,665 | 4,319,813 | 13 |
| 6 | Texas | 3,048,710 | 9,579,677 | 6 |
| 7 | Massachusetts | 2,805,346 | 5,148,578 | 9 |
| 8 | Indiana | 2,516,462 | 4,662,498 | 11 |
| 9 | Michigan | 2,420,982 | 7,823,194 | 7 |
| 10 | Iowa | 2,231,853 | 2,757,537 | 24 |
| 11 | Georgia | 2,216,331 | 3,943,116 | 16 |
| 12 | Kentucky | 2,147,174 | 3,038,156 | 22 |
| 13 | Wisconsin | 2,069,042 | 3,951,777 | 15 |
| 14 | Tennessee | 2,020,616 | 3,567,089 | 17 |
| 15 | North Carolina | 1,893,810 | 4,556,155 | 12 |
| 16 | New Jersey | 1,883,669 | 6,066,782 | 8 |
| 17 | Virginia | 1,854,184 | 3,966,949 | 14 |
| 18 | Alabama | 1,828,697 | 3,266,740 | 19 |
| 19 | Minnesota | 1,751,394 | 3,413,864 | 18 |
| 20 | Mississippi | 1,551,270 | 2,178,141 | 29 |
| 21 | California | 1,485,053 | 15,717,204 | 2 |
| 22 | Kansas | 1,470,495 | 2,178,611 | 28 |
| 23 | Louisiana | 1,381,625 | 3,257,022 | 20 |
| 24 | South Carolina | 1,340,316 | 2,382,594 | 26 |
| 25 | Arkansas | 1,311,564 | 1,786,272 | 31 |
| 26 | Maryland | 1,188,044 | 3,100,689 | 21 |
| 27 | Nebraska | 1,066,300 | 1,411,330 | 34 |
| 28 | West Virginia | 958,800 | 1,860,421 | 30 |
| 29 | Connecticut | 908,420 | 2,535,234 | 25 |
| 30 | Maine | 694,466 | 969,265 | 36 |

## Immigration

| | 1900 | 1960 |
|---|---|---|
| TOTAL ALL NATIONS | 448,572 | 265,398 |
| EUROPE | | |
| Austria-Hungary | 114,847 | * |
| Italy | 100,135 | 14,933 |
| Russia and Baltic States | 90,787 | 4,228 |
| Ireland (Northern & Eire) | 35,730 | 8,967 |
| Scandinavia | 31,151 | 6,379 |
| Germany | 18,507 | 31,768 |
| Great Britain | 12,509 | 23,363 |
| Romania | 6,459 | 993 |
| Portugal | 4,234 | 6,968 |
| Greece | 3,771 | 3,797 |

*Includes part or all of Austria, Hungary, Czechoslovakia, Poland*

| ASIA | | |
|---|---|---|
| Japan | 12,635 | 5,471 |
| Turkey | 3,962 | 674 |
| China | 1,247 | 3,681 |

## Immigration *(continued)*

| AMERICAS | 1900 | 1960 |
|---|---|---|
| West Indies and Miquelon | 4,656 | 14,052 |
| Canada | 396 | 30,990 |
| Mexico | 237 | 32,684 |
| South America | 124 | 13,048 |
| Central America | 42 | 6,661 |
| | | |
| AFRICA | 30 | 2,526 |
| AUSTRALIA AND NEW ZEALAND | 214 | 912 |

## Education

| | 1900 | 1960 |
|---|---|---|
| ELEMENTARY AND SECONDARY SCHOOLS | | |
| Enrollment | 16,855,000 | 41,778,000 |
| High school graduates | 95,000 | 1,864,000 |
| Total public school faculty | 423,000 | 1,387,000 |
| Average salary in public school | $325 | $5,174 |
| Cost per pupil | $17 | $472 |
| HIGHER EDUCATION | | |
| Enrollment | 238,000 | 3,216,000 |
| Undergraduate | 232,000 | 2,874,000 |
| Graduate school | 6,000 | 342,000 |
| Faculty | 23,868 | 380,554 |
| ILLITERACY PER CENT | 10.7% | 2.4% |

## Family Living

| | 1900 | 1960 |
|---|---|---|
| Average size of family | 4.7 persons | 3.7 persons |
| Total families | 16,188,000 | 45,062,000 |
| Total divorces | 56,000 | 393,000 |

## Health

| | 1900 | 1960 |
|---|---|---|
| AVERAGE LIFE EXPECTANCY | 47.3 years | 69.7 years |
| Male life expectancy | 46.3 years | 66.6 years |
| Female life expectancy | 48.3 years | 73.1 years |
| White life expectancy | 47.6 years | 70.6 years |
| Non-white life expectancy | 33.0 years | 63.6 years |
| | | |
| Birth rate per 1,000 | 32.3 | 23.7 |
| Death rate per 1,000 | 17.2 | 9.5 |
| Death rate per 1,000 under 1 year | 162.4 | 26.1 |
| | | |
| CAUSES OF DEATH PER 100,000 | | |
| Heart-Artery-Kidney diseases | 345.2 | 521.8 |
| Influenza and pneumonia | 202.2 | 37.3 |
| Tuberculosis | 194.4 | 6.1 |
| Gastro-intestinal diseases | 142.7 | 4.4 |
| Cancer | 64.0 | 149.2 |
| Diphtheria | 40.3 | less than 0.1 |
| Typhoid and paratyphoid | 31.3 | less than 0.1 |
| Malaria | 19.5 | less than 0.1 |
| Measles | 13.3 | 0.2 |
| Whooping cough | 12.2 | 0.1 |
| Suicide | 10.2 | 10.6 |
| Appendicitis | 6.7 | 1.0 |
| Childbirth | 5.9 | 0.9 |
| | | |
| Total motor vehicle deaths | under 100 | 38,137 |
| Total executions | 155 | 56 |
| Total lynchings | 115 | none recorded |

## Labor

| | 1900 | 1960 |
|---|---|---|
| TOTAL WORKING FORCE | 29,030,000 | 70,612,000 |
| Men working | 23,711,000 | 47,025,000 |
| Women working | 5,319,000 | 23,587,000 |
| Per cent unemployed | 5% | 5.6% |
| EMPLOYMENT BY MAJOR INDUSTRY | | |
| Agriculture | 10,710,000 | 4,256,000 |
| Manufacturing | 6,340,000 | 17,513,000 |
| Service | 3,210,000 | 5,470,000 |
| Trade, finance and real estate | 2,760,000 | 14,487,000 |
| Transportation and other utilities | 2,100,000 | 4,458,000 |
| Construction | 1,660,000 | 3,816,000 |
| Mining | 760,000 | 654,000 |
| Forestry and fisheries | 210,000 | 93,000 |

## LABOR (continued)

### SAMPLE OCCUPATIONS

| | 1900 | 1960 |
|---|---|---|
| Dressmakers (not factory) | 413,000 | 119,000 |
| Blacksmiths, forgemen and hammermen | 220,000 | 32,000 |
| Barbers and beauticians | 133,000 | 480,000 |
| Physicians | 131,000 | 229,000 |
| Bartenders | 89,000 | 172,000 |
| Milliners | 75,000 | 4,000 |
| Electricians | 51,000 | 337,000 |
| Telephone operators | 19,000 | 357,000 |
| Professional nurses (inc. students) | 12,000 | 640,000 |
| Newsboys | 7,000 | 190,000 |

### AVERAGE WAGE

| | 1900 | 1960 |
|---|---|---|
| Per week | $12.74 | $89.72 |
| Per hour | $ 0.22 | $ 2.26 |
| AVERAGE WORK WEEK (in hours) | 59.0 | 39.7 |

## Transportation

| | 1900 | 1960 |
|---|---|---|
| **RAILROADS** | | |
| Passenger miles | 16,038,000,000 | 21,284,000,000 |
| Freight ton miles | 141,597,000,000 | 575,360,000,000 |
| No. of companies | 1,224 | 407 |
| Steam locomotives | 37,463 | 374 |
| Electric locomotives | 200 | 498 |
| Diesel locomotives | none | 30,240 |
| **SHIPS** | | |
| Total commercial ships | 23,333 | 43,088 |
| Steam tonnage | 2,658,000 | 23,553,000 |
| Sail tonnage | 1,885,000 | 23,000 |
| **AUTOMOBILES** | | |
| Total registered cars | 8,000 | 61,682,000 |
| Total registered trucks and buses | none | 12,213,000 |
| Maximum record speed | 65.79 mph | 394.1 mph |
| Total miles of paved roads | under 150 | 3,546,000 |

| | 1902 | 1960 |
|---|---|---|
| **TROLLEY CARS** | | |
| Total miles of track | 22,577 | 2,196 |
| Vehicle miles | 1,144,000,000 | 100,700,000 |

## Business

| | 1900 | 1960 |
|---|---|---|
| GROSS NATIONAL PRODUCT | $16,800,000,000* | $502,600,000,000 |
| Goods | $8,420,000,000 | $257,100,000,000 |
| Services | $4,440,000,000 | $188,800,000,000 |
| Other | $3,890,000,000 | $56,700,000,000 |
| IMPORTS | $1,179,000,000 | $14,654,000,000 |
| EXPORTS | $1,686,000,000 | $20,550,000,000 |

*average over 5 year period 1897-1901

## BUSINESS (continued)

### TOP COMPANIES AND ASSETS

| | 1909* | 1960 |
|---|---|---|
| United States Steel Corp. | $1,804,000,000 | $4,781,000,000 |
| Standard Oil Co., New Jersey | 800,000,000 | 10,090,000,000 |
| American Tobacco Co. | 286,000,000 | 851,000,000 |
| Int'l Mercantile Marine Co. *now U.S. Lines Co.* | 192,000,000 | 40,000,000 |
| Amalgamated Copper Co. *now Anaconda Copper Co.* | 170,000,000 | 1,086,000,000 |
| Int'l Harvester Co. | 166,000,000 | 1,457,000,000 |
| Central Leather Co. | 138,000,000 | dissolved |
| Pullman Co. | 131,000,000 | 34,000,000 |
| Armour & Co. | 125,000,000 | 256,000,000 |
| American Sugar Co. | 124,000,000 | 197,000,000 |

*1900 figure not available

## Communication

| | 1900 | 1960 |
|---|---|---|
| **POST OFFICE** | | |
| Pieces of matter handled | 7,130,000,000 | 63,675,000,000 |
| **PRINTING** | | |
| New books published | 4,490 | 12,069 |
| Total daily newspapers | 2,226 | 1,763 |
| Circulation of daily newspapers | 15,102,000 | 58,882,000 |
| **TELEPHONE AND TELEGRAPH** | | |
| Telephones per 1,000 | 17.6 | 408.1 |
| Telegraph messages sent per 1,000 | 217.2 | 755.6 |

## Government

| | 1900 | 1960 |
|---|---|---|
| GROSS DEBT | $1,263,417,000 | $286,471,000,000 |
| TOTAL RECEIPTS | $567,241,000 | $77,763,000,000 |
| Internal revenue | $295,328,000 | $73,291,000,000 |
| Customs revenue | $233,165,000 | $1,105,000,000 |
| Miscellaneous | $38,748,000 | $4,062,000,000 |
| TOTAL EXPENDITURES | $520,861,000 | $76,539,000,000 |
| SURPLUS | $46,380,000 | $1,224,000,000 |
| TOTAL CIVILIAN EMPLOYEES | 239,476* | 2,430,000 |
| **SALARIES** | | |
| Member of Congress | $5,000 | $22,500 |
| Cabinet member | $8,000 | $25,000 |
| Vice President | $8,000 | $35,000 |
| President | $50,000 | $100,000 |

*1901 (1900 figure not available)

*Daytona Beach, Florida, about 1904.*

America
1900·1910

tastes good
because
it is good

13

*New York City, after 1900.*

*Company outing, Waukesha Beach, Wisconsin, 1908.*

*Delivering ice, Cleveland, around 1910.*

*Fourth of July, Nome, Alaska, 1901.*

*Lunchtime, Minnesota farm, about 1900.*

*The Erie Canal, Durhamville, New York, about 1905.*

*Cotton-marketing day, Marietta, Georgia, 1905.*

*The finish of a transcontinental auto tour, 1904.*

**READING THE WILL**

**THE INHERITANCE OF THE XX<sup>TH</sup> CENTURY**

*A feckless youth in sporty attire, the 20th Century whistles nonchalantly as he scans the mixed legacy of problems and assets bequeathed to him by the Old Century.*

# The Cocksure Era

*The will to grow was everywhere written large, and to grow at no matter what or whose expense.*

HENRY JAMES

It was a splendid time, a wonderful country. Most Americans felt that way as they welcomed the 20th Century, and many of them said so, with great animation and grandiose references to Peace, Prosperity and Progress.

From Senator Chauncey Depew of New York: "There is not a man here who does not feel 400 per cent bigger in 1900 than he did in 1896, bigger intellectually, bigger hopefully, bigger patriotically."

Depew's colleague, Mark Hanna of Ohio: "Furnaces are glowing, spindles are singing their song. Happiness comes to us all with prosperity."

The Reverend Newell Dwight Hillis of Brooklyn: "Laws are becoming more just, rulers humane; music is becoming sweeter and books wiser."

These statements set the mood for the first decade of the new century and won for the period several titles —the Age of Optimism, the Age of Confidence, the Age of Innocence. But another tag might have seemed more appropriate to an objective visitor from abroad: the Cocksure Era. For this was a time when Americans were optimistic and self-confident to an extreme; they did not merely hope for the best, they fully expected it. A welter of practical and moral problems—child labor, teeming slums, widespread offenses by corrupt politicians and ruthless corporations—could not shake the faith of Americans in the inevitability of their progress as individuals and as a nation. Most people automatically assumed that all problems would be solved in the normal course of events; meanwhile, the important thing was for a man to get ahead, to earn maximum returns from bountiful opportunities.

There was ample reason for high hopes and general satisfaction. The housewife found the stores well stocked and prices low: she could buy eggs for 12 cents a dozen, sirloin steak for 24 cents a pound, a turkey dinner for 20 cents. The farmer was doing well after some hard times in the '90s. For the businessman, taxes were minimal and trade was brisk; indeed, conditions were almost good enough to justify the Boston *Herald*'s verdict, "If one could not have made money this past year, his case is hopeless." Everyone was fascinated by the many useful devices coming to the fore: the telephone, the typewriter and the sewing machine, the self-binding harvester and even the automobile (fully 8,000 of these vehicles were registered by 1900). But to the thoughtful citizen, the surest portents of a brilliant future were the astonishing achievements of the recent American past.

In the 19th Century, American energy and individualism had written a national epic without historic parallel. A thin fringe of Eastern states with five million inhabitants had swelled into a continent-wide nation with a population of 76 million. In the 35 years since the Civil War, a predominantly agrarian country had vaulted from fourth place to first among the world's industrial powers; a loose collection of very different regions, permissively administered by the laissez-faire government, had been woven into a fairly homogeneous and interdependent unit by expanding railroad networks, lengthening newspaper chains and burgeoning techniques of mass production and nationwide marketing. And in just the past few years, the United States had fought and won an exhilarating war with Spain, emerging as a major military power with possessions and protectorates that sprawled from the Caribbean to the China Seas. The facts and figures—a veritable torrent of information on rich resources and soaring growth rates—promised that progress would continue at an accelerating speed.

Though no single fact could sum up America's past and present, the one that came closest was a casual item, appearing in the Census Bureau report for 1900, that brought brief fame to the small town of Columbus, Indiana. According to the report, the geographic center of population was now located near Columbus—a move of about 475 miles west since 1800. Implicit in the item were vast and ever-shifting patterns of migration: the arrival and dispersal of 19 million immigrants; the conquest of the western frontier; the rise of big cities where once had stood forests and prairies; the rise and decline of innumerable small towns—and, no less significant, the survival of countless towns and villages virtually unchanged in size and character, ideals and biases. In progressing from the good old days to complex modern times, America was changing faster than its people knew, but it was also remaining much the same.

Clearly each community, whether rural or urban, was a special case, subject to a unique combination of forces. Old boom towns such as Creede, Colorado, petered out along with their payloads, while a corona of new towns in Minnesota attested to the discovery of the Mesabi iron-ore range. The commercial success of furniture factories in Grand Rapids, Michigan, cut into the business

---

*God has marked the American people as His chosen nation to finally lead in the regeneration of the world. This is the divine mission of America, and it holds for us all the profit, all the glory, all the happiness possible to man. We are trustees of the world's progress, guardians of its righteous peace.*

SENATOR ALBERT J. BEVERIDGE OF INDIANA

---

of country cabinetmakers as far east as Litchfield, Connecticut; the displaced rural artisans drifted into the cities to seek new work. But the most far-reaching influence on the pattern of settlement was the railroads.

For countless communities, the route of a railroad made the difference between growth and decay. Along the 193,368 miles of track that crisscrossed America in 1900, hundreds of hamlets survived or were jerry-built in the middle of nowhere, because they were needed to service the panting locomotives, which had to take on water every 40 miles or so. These forlorn way stations gave birth to some particularly graphic American slang: "tank town," "whistle stop," "jerkwater." On the other hand, many thriving inland ports, such as Little Falls on the Erie Canal and Paducah on the Ohio River, saw their dreams of greatness crushed, and were reduced to provincial towns, as manufacturers shifted their shipments from barge and steamboat to the faster rail freights. Even celebrated ports on the Mississippi were affected; Cairo and Hannibal and other towns suffered population losses traceable in large degree to the rise of St. Louis as a major railroad center. The decline of the Mississippi traffic was sudden and steep. The lifetime of one former river-pilot, Mark Twain, embraced both the heyday and the twilight of the palatial stern-wheeler. "A strangely short life," said the author sadly, "for so magnificent a creature."

The statistics told an ominous story to rural America. While 60 per cent of the U.S. population in 1900 lived on farms or in communities with less than 2,500 inhabitants, that percentage represented a nationwide shrinkage over the previous three decades. Rural New England had long since lost much of its population to the cities and to the Midwest; in turn, the rural Midwest had begun losing population to the cities and to the West as early as the 1870s. A survey of 6,291 small towns in five Midwestern states for the decade ending in 1890 revealed that fully 3,144 communities had recorded appreciable losses in population. By 1908, the continuing decline of the small town was causing such concern that President Theodore Roosevelt set up a commission to make an investigation.

Nevertheless, magazine articles announcing "The Doom of the Small Town" proved premature. It was true that many young men, attracted by the opportunities and excitement of the cities, departed on that classic journey by day coach to make a name or a fortune on the urban frontier; many rural towns, stripped of their most promising people, became, as an unfriendly observer put it, "fished-out ponds populated chiefly by bullheads and suckers." But at the same time many country towns attained a kind of stability and fulfilled useful purposes even in eclipse. Resolutely conservative in all things, they served as restraints on the pace of progress, as strongholds of the stern old-time religion, as custodians of homely virtues and ideals taught generations by McGuffey's *Readers*, as islands of security and leisure amid the hustle and hazards of modern times. In rural America God was surely in His heaven and all was right with the world.

Nostalgia for the country hometown staked a permanent claim on the American imagination. The close-knit relationships of rural life—that sense of belonging which author Zona Gale glorified under the name of "Togetherness"—cast a spell on even those who had never lived in a small town. Five former country boys, yearning for lost Togetherness in Chicago, manufactured an urban substitute in 1905; they founded the Rotary Club, whose membership grew in coldly impersonal cities from coast to coast. Many a man made a sentimental journey to his rural hometown, there to savor again its changeless peace and order, the kindness and informality of its people.

Despite the appeal of country towns, the cities grew ever more populous. They received a vastly disproportionate share of the 8.8 million immigrants who arrived in America during the decade. The newcomers, most of them poor Italians and Russians and Poles and Jews, found plenty of work in the mining towns of Pennsylvania and West Virginia, in the sweatshops of New York and Chicago, in the mills and plants of Pitts-

---

*The rights and interests of the laboring man will be protected and cared for—not by labor agitators, but by the Christian men to whom God in His infinite wisdom has given the control of the property interests of the country.*

GEORGE F. BAER, PRESIDENT, PHILADELPHIA & READING RAILWAY

---

burgh, St. Louis and Cincinnati. Here the newcomers also found plenty of countrymen; immigration in the 19th Century had been so heavy that one third of the people in the United States in 1900 were foreign born or were the children of foreign born.

The cities bulged upward in skyscrapers and tall apartment houses, and outward in jumbles of slums and mansions, grimy factories and cheap-Jack entertainment centers. The population of three cities—New York, Chicago and Philadelphia—had topped the million mark by 1900. Secondary cities—Cleveland, St. Louis and Los Angeles—were much smaller but growing fast.

Growth rates could be used to form a general notion of the city's future, but they were inaccurate indicators. Nevertheless, at the turn of the century, when civic pride and boisterous optimism inspired a spate of fu-

*A futuristic drawing done in 1900 portrays the New York City of 1999 crammed with skyscrapers, overflown by airships and served by a network of bridges.*

turistic articles and illustrations (left), local experts applied the figures with great self-confidence. Various New Yorkers, attempting to calculate the population of their metropolis in the year 1999, arrived by way of the same statistics at predictions ranging anywhere from eight to 45 million. One oracle, noting that automobiles were shorter than horse-drawn vehicles and that auto engines were cleaner than horses, reached the wild conclusion that the cities of tomorrow would have immaculate streets and no traffic jams.

No one, not even the most imaginative prophet, could have predicted in 1900 what was about to happen to a sunbaked Oklahoma hamlet known locally as Tulsey town. Tulsey town itself might well have looked to the past rather than the future. Long an Indian meeting place, it was a small cowtown in 1900; its population was only 1,340, and the town consisted of a single dirt street lined with ramshackle buildings. According to the local press, freight-car business for the first week of 1900 was far from encouraging: "Receipts: one car bran; shipments: two cars hogs, one car sand, one car mules." The big story of the day was half business, half social event: Chief Frank Corndropper was soon to give his daughter Mary in marriage and to receive in return the groom's gift of several hundred ponies.

But 18 months later, Tulsey town—Tulsa—struck oil. By 1910, the population had soared to 18,182; 14 years later Tulsa would be a prosperous city of 110,000 inhabitants. Not everybody got rich, of course. But the career of one man was a fair index to Tulsa's success. James J. McGraw arrived as a poor boy in the land rush of '93, and he rose with the town to become president of a bank, ensconced in offices in a 12-story skyscraper, doing an annual business of $40 million.

Even more spectacular was the growth of a planned city on the banks of the Calumet River in northern Indiana. In 1905, the site was 12.5 square miles of wasteland—rolling sand dunes covered with scrub oak. But late that year the city's namesake, Judge Elbert H. Gary, chairman of the board of United States Steel, poked a manicured finger at a map and told his directors, "This will be our metropolis. We'll build near the railroad junction of Chicago, where acres of land can be had almost for the asking, midway between the ore regions of the North and the coal regions of the South and East." The analysis was faultless and the city of Gary was christened before it was born.

The company's efforts soon proved once again that nothing could prevent American money and technology from working miracles. A bothersome river was moved a hundred yards. Great mechanical diggers chewed a mile-long harbor back from Lake Michigan; the major site was raised 15 feet with fill pumped in from the lake bottom. As railroad connections were forged, the jagged outlines of steel mills and foundries and tin-plate plants rose against the sky. The final product was ready in July 1908. With proper ceremony, the first ore boat unloaded its cargo in Gary harbor and set the mills thundering. By 1910, Gary was an efficient corporative barony with a population of 16,802. That was Progress.

Or was it? A world of subtle difference separated true progress from mere change, and more and more Americans pondered the dimensions of that world as the decade wore on. Were urban phenomena like Gary and Tulsa and New York better places of habitation than the small town of Columbus, Indiana, or were they—as several grimly realistic novelists insisted—misbegotten work centers whose ugliness appalled the eye and whose labors crushed the human spirit with the mindless repetition of a single act on the production line? Did all their labor-saving, product-multiplying devices really improve the quality of American life? And was the work and wealth of modern industry divided equitably?

On this last count, the opponents of the status quo had a great deal to say. Muckraking journalists published angry exposés and backed their demands for reform with disturbing statistics. The average annual earnings of industrial workers in 1900 was a subsistence wage of less than $490; included in that figure were some 1.7 million children who labored for as little as 25 cents a day. One citizen out of eight lived in dire poverty in festering slums and perished of disease at about twice the rate of modest-income groups. In short, the reformers charged that labor was being exploited by an oligarchy of capitalists who lived in idle ostentation on annual incomes of many millions. The Very Rich said little in rebuttal, but one plutocrat did their cause no good by declaring arrogantly, "We own America; we got it, God knows how, but we intend to keep it."

Along these lines a battle was joined that would develop into a national crisis of social conscience. America's sense of justice and humanity, its treasured precept of equal opportunity for all, its jealously guarded tradition of free enterprise—all were called sharply into question. A free-swinging article in the Atlanta *Constitution* went so far as to say: "Government is no longer a vehicle for the enforcement of human rights but an agency for the furtherance of commercial interests."

Slowly, painfully, citizens faced up to the great civic work of 20th Century America: to make government more responsive to the needs and aspirations of the people; to reduce the discrepancies between lofty ideals and expedient practices, between good intentions and driving ambitions. That work had barely begun when the decade drew to a close. But it did begin. And *that* was Progress.

Yet if the sense of urgency was slow to grow, it was only natural to the time. For the great majority of people, the decade was a golden interlude, a long, comfortable moment before the good young days vanished completely and modern times arrived at full tide. Americans believed the judgments that confirmed their personal experience: That the human condition "is immensely improved and continually improving"; that "To stay in place in this country, you must keep moving"; that the average U.S. citizen possessed, and should enjoy, "the large cheerful average of health and success." It was generally true. Life for Americans from 1900 to 1910 was mellow and quite secure, full of vigor, savor and fascination. All they had to do was go out and live it.

*A cartoonist's fantasy in 1901 included, among other items, 150-mile-per-hour trains and home ice-making machines—all by the end of the 20th Century.*

# A Man's World

*The men of the Trident Boat Club of Manchester, New Hampshire, meet for an impromptu band concert.*

# The Master Sex

*The relative positions to be assumed by man and woman in the working out of our civilization were assigned long ago by a higher intelligence than ours.*

GROVER CLEVELAND

In any confrontation between the sexes, it was a foregone conclusion that men would come out ahead. For one thing, according to the 1900 census, men outnumbered women by more than a million and a half. But masculine supremacy went far beyond mere numbers. Like ex-President Grover Cleveland, every red-blooded American male was convinced that the sex he belonged to was innately superior.

The entire country, in fact, from the logging camps of Oregon to the U.S. Senate—with its convenient cuspidors—was seemingly arranged by men for their own satisfaction. Men ran the nation's business, cast its votes and produced most of its art and literature. They were, in theory at least, complete masters of their households, dispensing justice and wisdom to their families like Oriental potentates.

Along with their exalted status, men reserved special rights and privileges. Not only did they ban ladies from voting booths, they also kept them out of clubs, restaurants, saloons and tobacco shops. In some states an unescorted female might, by law, be refused a meal at a restaurant or a room at a hotel, and in 1904 one particularly audacious young lady was arrested and put in jail in New York City for smoking a cigarette in public.

While men called the tune, they also worked hard to pay the piper. Most men labored at least 10 hours a day, six days a week. An office worker was usually at his stool by eight o'clock, a factory hand at his bench by seven. Both would remain there until five-thirty or six, when they would trudge home to pipe, slippers and the affectionate ministrations of wife and children. All for an average weekly pay of less than $12.

In the confident mood of the first decade, however, most men were robustly certain that the opportunity to strike it rich lay just around the corner. With hard work and a bit of luck they might, like the Horatio Alger heroes, rise from clerk to president of the company. As good men, in an age of male superiority, they deserved no less.

But whether he was a bank teller or a board chairman, the American male usually managed to fit himself out in a style that was suitable to a member of the privileged sex. He acquired clothing and accessories—such as the fancy shirts, silk hats, matchboxes and other articles shown at right and on the following pages—that solidly proclaimed his membership in the world of men.

*Sartorial artifacts of the men's world of 1900 included detachable collar and cuffs, pocket watches, a silk hat, eyeglasses in a silver case and a silver-headed cane.*

## The Dandy's Gear

*The average man used an impressive array of grooming devices (above), to keep his hair sleek, his face smooth and his moustache trim. The most essential item was a folding, straight-edged razor with a wood or ivory handle (foreground, on top of mirror), which he honed on a leather strop (left, hanging from oak shaving cabinet). Using a brush of soft badger hair (on cup, foreground), he worked up a lather in a china shaving mug, which was often ornamented with a personal insignia. The mugs in the cabinet include one bearing the owner's initials, another (middle of the center shelf) decorated with the emblem of the owner's fraternal organization, the Elks. After-shave lotion was kept in colorful glass bottles; cologne bottles were occasionally protected in boxwood cases (near blue after-shave bottles). For the hair and moustache, there was pomade (top shelf, at left)—and sometimes hair dye to preserve the youthful look that all men desired.*

## The Master's Toys

*Most men's pleasures were fairly simple—a good cigar, a tot of whiskey, a poker game with friends—but the paraphernalia that went with them (right) was often elaborate. Cigar cutters took the shape of guillotines (rear center). There were oil lamps that both clipped and lighted a fragrant Havana (center, inscribed with an ad for Blaine Cigars). The majority of men chewed plug tobacco, and prided themselves on their talent for scoring a bull's-eye in a shiny brass spittoon (right, holding cards). But cigars and pipes, from simple briars to elegantly carved meerschaums (foreground), were almost as popular. Whiskey was often kept in fancy crystal decanters that could be locked into a portable case (right, rear), or in handy breast-pocket flasks shaped like cigars (center foreground). Poker chips and counters for various other card and dice games ranged from conventional disks to rectangular counters and ivory fish (right foreground).*

*Rudy Sohn's Barber Shop in Junction City, Kansas, with its reclining chairs and rows of shaving mugs on the wall, exuded an air of solid, masculine comfort.*

## Manly Retreats

"There is something mentally enervating in feminine companionship," advised *The Cosmopolitan* in 1905, and so "the genuine man feels that he must go off alone or with other men, out in the open air, as it were, roughing it among the rough, as a mental tonic." The spirit, if not the letter, of that statement was dogma at the time. Most men sought the society of other males in less rugged circumstances, in the comfortable, for-men-only atmosphere of barbershops, clubs and saloons. A turn-of-the-century barbershop was much more than a place to get a haircut. It was a retreat where, amid the reek of cigar fumes and bay rum, men would congregate to browse through the spicy pages of the *Police Gazette*, ogle the ladies who hurried past the door, and wait for a 15-cent shave.

Even more impregnable to women were the men's clubs. For the rich and wellborn, there were such exclusive establishments as New York City's august Union League Club, whose major asset, according to one member, was the fact that "no women, no dogs, no Democrats, no reporters" could be found there. But most clubs were a good deal more proletarian. The average man could join sporting societies, volunteer fire companies, municipal bands and marching societies, and gourmandizing fraternities with such fancy names as the Honorable John McSorley Pickle, Beefsteak, Baseball Nine and Chowder Club, which held raucous clambakes on an island in the East River in New York.

The most democratic gathering places of all were the saloons. There were at least 100,000 of these in the country, supplied by 3,000 breweries and distilleries. It is a fact of record that in Boston and Chicago, half the male population paid a daily visit to favored neighborhood bars. Part of the saloon's appeal was camaraderie, but the main attraction was the whiskey. So important was this commodity that on one occasion, when a supplier drew up to the door of a saloon with 20 large kegs of whiskey and a few small sacks of flour, one customer dryly commented, "Now what in hell does he think we're going to do with all that flour."

*The Cosmopolitan Saloon in Telluride, Colorado, featured roulette and a mahogany bar, which served whiskey as raw and rugged as the men who drank it.*

*With an appropriate set of props—shotguns, rifles, bottles, hounds and a papier-mâché rabbit—the Skeet Club of Fall Creek, Wisconsin, sits for an official portrait.*

*Number One fire-eaters, members of the fire department of Woodbine, New Jersey, assemble around patriarchal chief.*

*Lodge brothers of the Independent Order of Odd Fellows at Kerkhoven, Minnesota, display their ceremonial regalia.*

*Volunteer fire companies, like this one from Longmont, Colorado, often spent as much time training for races (above) with other towns as drilling for fires.*

*Crowned in laurel wreaths, an Olympian assemblage honors the theatrical promoter Harrison Grey Fiske (front row, third from left) at a lush dinner about 1901.*

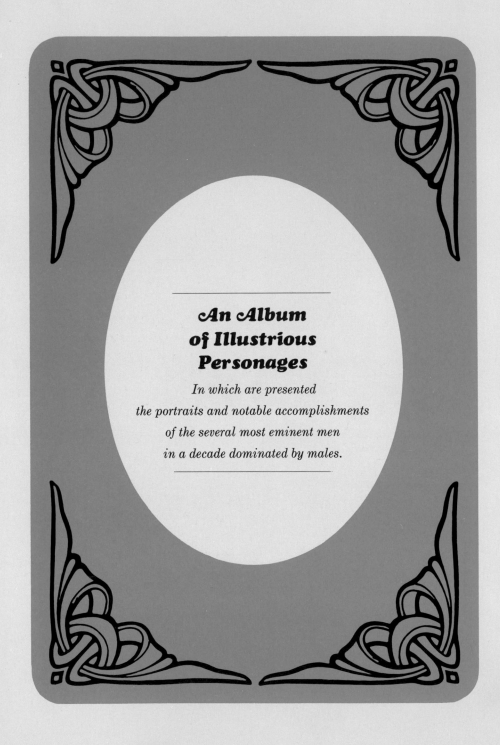

## *An Album of Illustrious Personages*

*In which are presented
the portraits and notable accomplishments
of the several most eminent men
in a decade dominated by males.*

*Arctic explorer* Robert E. Peary drove a dogsled 400 miles from his ship to become the first man to stand at the North Pole. He reached it on April 6, 1909, in cold so intense that a flask of brandy carried under his parka froze solid. He marked the spot with the Stars and Stripes and the colors of the Red Cross, of the Navy League, of the Daughters of the American Revolution and of Delta Kappa Epsilon (his college fraternity). Returning to civilization, Peary cabled his wife: "Have made good at last. I have the old Pole."

**Military man** *General Leonard Wood was the stern symbol of a strong America during the country's colonial expansion. First a practicing physician, then winner of a Congressional Medal of Honor in action against the Apaches in 1886, he later commanded U.S. troops during the Spanish-American War. Subsequently, as military governor of Cuba, he directed the fight against yellow fever and provided for the uplift of the lives, education and government of the native population with a healthy serving of Anglo-Saxon civilization.*

**Press czar** *William Randolph Hearst ushered in mass-circulation newspapers with sensationalism. After initial success with the San Francisco "Examiner," he bought the failing New York "Morning Journal" in 1895 and made it the model of yellow journalism. Through the lavish use of photographs, splashy headlines, colored comics, a saber-rattling editorial policy and some juicy scandals, he soon upped its circulation to an unprecedented 1.5 million copies—thus bringing more news to more Americans than any publisher before him.*

**Minority champion** *William Jennings Bryan led the underdog Democratic Party for almost two decades with a combination of shrewd cloakroom deals and compelling oratory. He ran three times for President but was beaten by Republicans McKinley and Taft. Even in defeat he was a formidable fighter for such lost causes as silver-based currency, attacking the gold standard with broadsides of Biblical locution: "You shall not press down upon the brow of labor this crown of thorns; you shall not crucify mankind upon a cross of gold."*

**Beau ideal** *Richard Harding Davis personified masculinity and derring-do. Novelist, journalist, man-about-town, he was known as the top war correspondent of his era. However, his flair for dramatic reporting was more than matched by his dashing appearance—square-jawed, clean shaven, stylish even on the battlefield. His personality was a strange mixture of vanity and self-mockery. "What I like most in men," he said, is the ability "to sit opposite a mirror at dinner and not look in it"—an ability he himself did not possess.*

**Kingpin banker** *J. Pierpont Morgan was the most powerful financier in American history. The very "embodiment of power and purpose," according to a fellow businessman, he used his uncanny business sense and awesome presence to create the world's largest corporation, U.S. Steel. Later, he singlehandedly saved the country from financial collapse in the panic of 1907—by holding 125 leading New York financiers under lock and key in his palatial library near Madison Avenue until they produced the capital to stave off disaster.*

**Leading educator** *Booker T. Washington rose from slavery to found America's first college for Negro teachers, Tuskegee Institute in Alabama. Though resentment against Negro advancement ran high, President Theodore Roosevelt openly described the Negro leader as the South's most distinguished citizen. When the President asked him to dinner at the White House, most Southerners were scandalized. In the face of such bigotry, Washington felt no bitterness. "I shall never permit myself to stoop so low as to hate any man," he said.*

**The man of the decade,** *President Theodore Roosevelt was the living embodiment of the optimism and energy of the country's mood. During his seven and a half years of vigorous, personal leadership, from 1901 to 1909, he wielded the powers of the Presidency as no man had done before. Roosevelt called his crusade the Square Deal, and the people loved it. They loved him for himself, too. "I have never known another person so vital," wrote author and editor William Allen White, speaking for the nation, "nor another man so dear."*

# The American Colossus

Among the many notable men of his time, Theodore Roosevelt—soldier, statesman, author, adventurer and advocate of the strenuous life—stood out above all others and left an unmistakable stamp on America. It was not physical stature, certainly, that made Roosevelt appear such a dominant figure. Dumpy-looking, his eyes heavily spectacled, a toothy smile protruding from under a walrus moustache, he cut an almost comical figure, somewhat like a cartoonist's rendition of an early Colonel Blimp. Neither was he a giant merely because of his birth—he was the son of a patrician Dutch family from New York City; nor because of his political office, the Presidency. It was rather the dynamic force of his presence, together with his awesome energy, that made the ebullient Teddy stand larger in people's minds than any other man of his time. "His personality so crowds the room," said a friend, "that the walls are worn thin and threaten to burst outward."

Everything about T.R. seemed bigger than life. He drank his coffee, with seven lumps of sugar, from a cup that, according to his eldest son, Teddy Jr., was "more in the nature of a bathtub." When he spoke, with a high-pitched, staccato bark, he became a "human volcano, roaring as only a human volcano can roar!—leading the laughter and singing and shouting, like a boy out of school, pounding the table with both noisy fists." He walked with such a fierce, determined stride that most people had to break into a dogtrot to keep up with him. "I always believe in going hard at everything," he wrote his son Kermit. Nothing dampened his enthusiasm for rough-and-tumble. During a fox hunt in 1885, he fell off his horse and broke his arm. He remounted, finished the hunt, went out to dinner in the evening and the next day tramped through the woods for three hours. "I like to drink the wine of life with brandy in it," he said.

This same unflagging vitality drove Roosevelt to the front line of public life. At age 24, he leaped into politics as a crusading Republican state assemblyman from New York City, determined to clean up political abuses in both parties. As New York City's police commissioner, he packed a pistol and patrolled the city streets to make sure his policemen kept busy catching criminals. With the outbreak of the Spanish-American War in 1898, he traded in his job as Assistant Secretary of the Navy to lead a volunteer cavalry regiment, the Rough Riders, in a daredevil charge up San Juan Hill in Cuba. "I don't want to be in office during war," he said; "I want to be at the front."

Teddy's swashbuckling approach to public life often infuriated old-line politicians. The Republican national chairman, Mark Hanna, called him "that damned cowboy," and on the eve of T.R.'s election as Vice President under William McKinley in 1900, Hanna exclaimed in dismay, "Don't any of you realize there's only one life between that madman and the Presidency?"

Only six months after McKinley's inauguration, Hanna's fears were realized. In September 1901, an assassin's bullet took McKinley's life, and Teddy rattled by wagon down the trail from a mountain lodge in the Adirondacks to become, at age 42, the youngest President in American history.

Roosevelt plunged into the adventure of being President with the enthusiasm of a small boy embarking on a hayride. "You must always remember," said a British diplomat, "that the President is about six." But Teddy's accomplishments were man-sized. He acted to curb the power of the nation's huge trade monopolies and financial trusts—"malefactors of great wealth," as he called them. He arbitrated labor disputes, reformed railroad rates, pushed through a pure food and drug law and plucked 148 million acres of forest land from under the noses of lumbermen to create national parks. Wielding his famous "big stick" in foreign affairs, he battered down stubborn diplomatic obstacles to build the Panama Canal.

Inevitably, Roosevelt's energetic policies made him enemies. But though T.R. claimed he did not "care a rap for 'popularity' as such," the American people refused to believe him. His public appearances drew enthusiastic crowds. "Whenever he is in the neighborhood," wrote a commentator, "the public can no more look the other way than a small boy can turn his head from a circus parade followed by a steam calliope." Campaigning in 1904 on his platform of a Square Deal for every American, Teddy was re-elected for a second term by the largest plurality amassed until then by a Presidential candidate.

Roosevelt was more than an energetic but shallow demagogue in a cowboy hat. His intellectual interests seemed to touch the whole spectrum of human knowledge. "Whether the subject of the moment was political economy, the Greek drama, tropical fauna or flora, the Irish sagas, protective coloration in nature, metaphysics, the technique of football, or postfuturist painting," wrote the English statesman Viscount Lee, "he was equally at home with the experts." T.R. was himself such an au-thority on North American animal life that the professional zoologists at the Smithsonian Institution once called on him to identify a mystifying specimen of mammal in their collection.

Roosevelt's passion for reading was virtually insatiable. He consumed books at the rate of two or three a day, and he himself wrote 24 of them—histories, biographies, descriptions of cattle ranching and big game hunting, scholarly studies on natural history, speeches, magazine articles and newspaper editorials. Sometimes his writing took on a rather moralistic tone; a friend once said, "If there is one thing more than any other for which I admire you, Theodore, it is your original discovery of the Ten Commandments." But the following excerpts, despite a certain pompous sense of right, reveal the determination, the vigor and the intelligence that made up the spirit of the decade's biggest man.

---

*Having been a sickly boy, with no natural bodily prowess, and having lived much at home, I was at first quite unable to hold my own when thrown into contact with other boys of rougher antecedents. I was nervous and timid. Yet from reading of the people I admired I felt a great admiration for men who were fearless and who could hold their own in the world, and I had a great desire to be like them.*

*I am only an average man but, by George, I work harder at it than the average man.*

*It was still the Wild West in those days, the far West. We knew toil and hardship and hunger and thirst; and we saw men die violent deaths as they worked among the horses and cattle, or fought evil feuds with one another; but we felt the beat of hardy life in our veins, and ours was the glory of work and the joy of living.*

*I have scant use for the type of sportsmanship which consists merely in looking on at the feats of someone else.*

*There are no words that can tell the hidden spirit of the wilderness, that can reveal its mystery, its melancholy, and its charm. There is delight in the hardy life of the open, in long rides rifle in hand, in the thrill of the fight with dangerous game. Apart from this, yet mingled with it, is the strong attraction of the silent places, of the large tropic moons, and the splendor of the new stars; where the wanderer sees the awful glory of sunrise and sunset in the wide waste spaces of the earth, unworn of man, and changed only by the slow change of the ages through time everlasting.*

*We demand that big business give the people a square deal; in return we must insist that when any one engaged in big business honestly endeavors to do right he shall himself be given a square deal.*

*There is a homely adage which runs, "Speak softly and carry a big stick; you will go far."*

*Do not hit at all if it can be avoided, but never hit softly.*

*I wish to preach, not the doctrine of ignoble ease, but the doctrine of the strenuous life, the life of toil and effort, of labor and strife; to preach that highest form of success which comes, not to the man who desires mere easy peace, but to the man who does not shrink from danger, or from bitter toil, and who out of these wins the splendid ultimate triumph.*

*The White House is a bully pulpit.*

*For unflagging interest and enjoyment, a household of children, if things go reasonably well, certainly makes all other forms of success and achievement lose their importance by comparison.*

*Roosevelt sits for a 1903 family portrait with his wife, Edith, and children (from left): Quentin, 5; Ted, 15; Archie, 9; Alice, 19; Kermit, 13; and Ethel, 11.*

## Father of the First Family

Despite his eagerness for action and adventure, Teddy Roosevelt, like most other males of the decade, was very much a family man. He had six children, whom he managed to line up for the solemn portrait above. But the normal mood of the first family was about as sedate as a public school recess. There were baseball games on the White House lawn, tag in the hallways and a menagerie of assorted pets that included dogs, rabbits, flying squirrels, a badger and a small black bear. According to one seasoned retainer, it was "the wildest scramble in the history of the White House."

Roosevelt, far from restraining the activities of his children, often took part himself. He engaged them in wrestling bouts, pillow fights and football games. While at Sagamore Hill, the Roosevelt summer home near New York City, he took them on tramps through the woods and joined them in "romps" in the hayloft, although he admitted that it seemed "rather odd for a stout, elderly President to be bouncing over hay-ricks."

Roosevelt's constant delight in the doings of his offspring is reflected in his letters and other writings. The excerpts that accompany the photographs on the following pages reveal a fatherly pride that sometimes eclipsed even his pride in his wide-ranging public achievements.

"I don't think that any family has ever enjoyed the White House more than we have," Roosevelt wrote. Above, the two youngest children, Archie and Quentin, indulge in a favorite pastime—standing reveille with the White House guards.

Quentin, the baby, shows his pony to a White House officer. "He had one tumble," wrote T.R., "which, he remarked philosophically, did not hurt him any more than when I whacked him with a sofa cushion in one of our pillow fights."

Archie, "a most warm-hearted, loving, cunning little goose," was considered to be the best-natured and most outgoing of the rambunctious Roosevelt brood. He had hundreds of friends of all ages, including this solemn White House sentry.

"Archie and Quentin are great playmates," their father wrote of the two youngsters, who here try photography. "Quenty-quee has cast off the trammels of the nursery and become a most fearless though very good-tempered little boy."

*Of the six children, the most willful were the girls. Before one stint of baby-sitting with his younger daughter, Ethel, Roosevelt wrote in mock despair, "I have gloomy forebodings that after a brief struggle Ethel will take care of me."*

*Kermit, here holding his terrier, Allan, was a dreamy-eyed, introspective boy. When still very young, he was entranced by the evening sky and kept asking T.R., who he thought could do anything, to "get the moon, Father," and bring it to him.*

*Alice, the elder daughter, led such an active social life that T.R. complained she "only makes her appearance well after noon having been up until all hours dancing the night before."*

*Like the others, Ted, the eldest boy, loved pets. One of his favorites was a large bird named Eli, "the most gorgeous macaw," which his father claimed had "a bill that I think could bite through boiler plate."*

Archie's favorite mascot was a badger named Josiah. When not holding Josiah on his lap, Archie would wear out his stockings crawling after the pet, "whose temper," wrote the President, "was short but whose nature was fundamentally friendly."

The antics of Quentin and Archie, below, blowing soap bubbles on the lawn at Sagamore Hill, never ceased to delight the President. "Archie and Quentin are just as cunning as they can be," he commented in a glow of fatherly affection.

*Quentin, like his older brothers, was constantly acquiring pets, including a hutchful of rabbits, which, his father noted, "he brought in while we were at lunch yesterday, explaining that they were 'the valuablest kind, with pink eyes.'"*

*"There could be no healthier and pleasanter place in which to bring up children than that nook of old-time America around Sagamore Hill," wrote T. R., who joins in a football game at the country place that served as the summer White House.*

*Immigrants with baggage and identification tags land on Ellis Island, New York.*

The Newcomers

# The Immigrants' Ordeal

*Give me your tired, your poor, your huddled masses yearning to breathe free. Send . . . the homeless, tempest-tossed, to me, I lift my lamp beside the golden door!*

INSCRIPTION ON THE STATUE OF LIBERTY

*The scum of creation has been dumped on us. The most dangerous and corrupting hordes of the Old World have invaded us. The vice and crime which they have planted in our midst are sickening and terrifying.*

NATIVE-BORN POLITICIAN THOMAS WATSON

"Becoming an American," wrote a grateful but case-hardened immigrant, "is a spiritual adventure of the most volcanic variety." Heedless of such cautionings, some nine million immigrants came knocking at America's "golden door" between 1900 and 1910. Many were so poor that they could barely scrape together their fare in steerage—sums as small as $12 for the voyage from Italy. But all were irresistibly drawn by the conviction that in America they would find what the old country had denied them.

What they found in America severely tested the immigrants' faith—and their courage and stamina as well. For most of the newcomers, the ordeal of Americanization began on a bleak scrap of real estate in New York harbor, Ellis Island. In 1907, more than a million immigrants poured through the island's overtaxed processing facilities. Once admitted to the "Land of Opportunity," most newcomers were doomed to years of toil (12-hour days and six- or seven-day weeks), at subsistence pay (an average of less than $12.50 a week), in the garment-making sweatshops of New York, in the coal mines of Wilkes-Barre, in the spinning mills of Fall River and the grimy factories and slaughterhouses of Pittsburgh, Chicago and other Midwestern cities.

Though the immigrants were welcomed by Americans of good will, they also met with plain and fancy prejudice. Xenophobic natives ridiculed their alien ways, and regarded them as subhuman animals. Men as influential as Senator Henry Cabot Lodge lent prestige to bigotry by insisting that the latter-day immigrants were inferior peoples whose prolific issue threatened the very foundations of Anglo-American civilization. No less a savant than Francis A. Walker, president of the Massachusetts Institute of Technology, was so seized by prejudice that he pronounced the newcomers "beaten men from beaten races; representing the worst failures in the struggle for existence. They have none of the ideas and aptitudes which belong to those who are descended from the tribes that met under the oak trees of old Germany to make laws and choose chieftains."

Disillusioned by bigotry and poverty, many immigrants gave up and returned home; 395,000 departed in 1908 alone. But the vast majority persevered. "Their hearts," said sociologist Charles B. Spahr, "cannot be alienated. The ideals, the opportunities of our democracy change the immigrants into a new order of men."

*Mother and child, awaiting admission on Ellis Island, New York, are marked as immigrants by peasant garb—and the expression of hope, fear and stoic patience.*

Among the hordes to arrive in America in that climactic year of immigration, 1907, was a small boy of 10 from Italy, Edward Corsi, who later became U.S. Commissioner of Immigration and Naturalization for New York. Corsi's tour of duty as an official on Ellis Island kept fresh the memory of his own childhood arrival there; years later he recalled *(below)* the October day that brought him and his family from shipboard in the haze-hung harbor to their new home in an East Side tenement.

---

*M*ountains!" *I cried to my brother. "Look at them!" "They're strange," he said. "Why don't they have snow on them?" He was craning his neck and standing on tiptoe to stare through the haze at the New York skyline.*

*A small boat, the "General Putnam" of the Immigration Service, carried us from the pier to Ellis Island. We took our places in the long line and went submissively through the routine of answering interpreters' questions and receiving medical examinations. We were in line early so we avoided the necessity of staying overnight, an ordeal which my mother had long been dreading. Soon we were permitted to pass through America's gateway.*

*Crossing the harbor on the ferry, I was first struck by the fact that American men did not wear beards. In contrast with my own countrymen I thought they looked almost like women. I felt we were superior to them. I saw my first negro.*

*Carrying our baggage, we walked across lower Manhattan and then climbed the steps leading to one of these marvellous trains. On this train I saw a Chinaman, queue and all! It had been a day of breath-taking surprises. I decided that anything might be true in this strange country.*

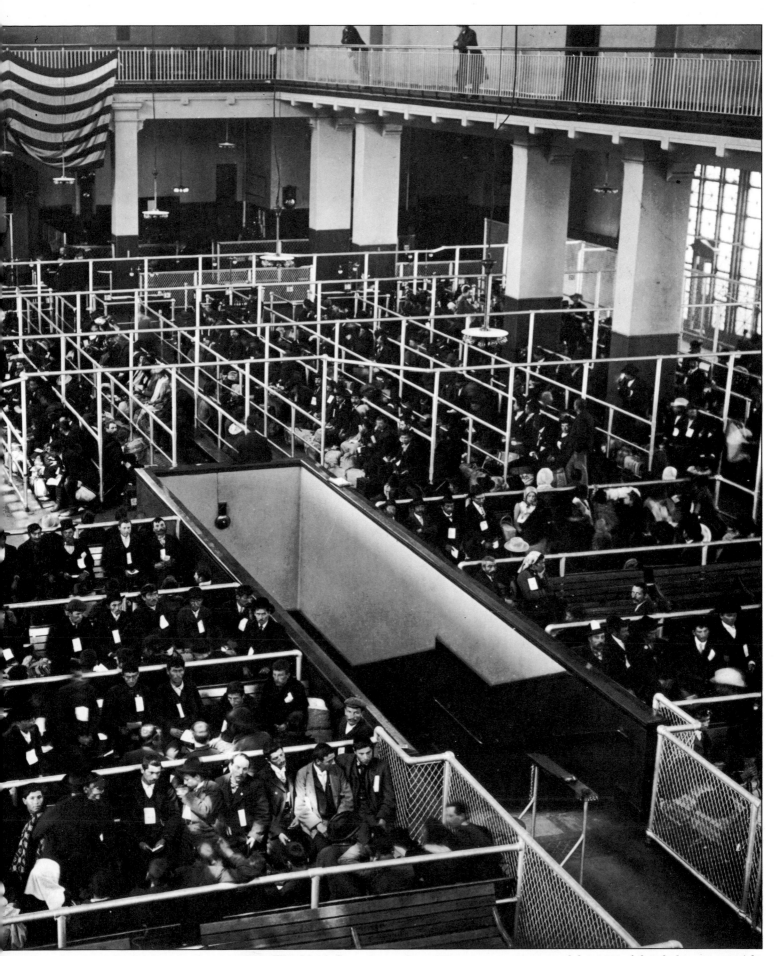

*Penned up in national groups, immigrants wait on Ellis Island. On an average day, 4,000 newcomers were processed, but 2,000 of them had to stay overnight.*

## Old World Beauties Greeted by American Bachelors

Under banner headlines like the one above, newspapers from coast to coast spread the joyful word that on September 27, 1907, a steamship had docked in New York with a spectacular cargo from Europe—1,002 unmarried girls. The Old World beauties came ashore to a hectic welcome. As photographers recorded their smiles *(right)*, the ladies were besieged by a crowd of bachelors and regaled by a band playing "Cupid's Garden" and "I Want You, Honey, Yes I Do." Here, in excerpts from the New York *World*, are details of the happy landing.

*No marriage mart of the Orient where brides were merchandise ever presented so bewitching a picture as the decks of the "Baltic" yesterday when 1002 beauties, colleens from Ireland, lasses from Scotland, maidens from Wales, girls from England and blondes from Scandinavia, rosy, dimpled and roguish eyed, marriageable every one, stood there, fascinated by their first glimpse of the New World.*

*"I like tall men and blondes," said Susan Thompson frankly, and then her companions all screamed and Susan laughed until she could hardly speak. "I have read much about Americans making good husbands."*

*Miss Agnes McGirr's home is in Edinburgh. "I want a man with dark hair," she chirped. "A city man? No, a farmer. A man who is making $1000 a year will do. That isn't too much to ask in this country is it? How old? Thirty. He has some sense, then."*

*"They tell me," remarked Nellie O'Brien from Loch Crae,* *Tipperary, "that there are no men in Pittsburgh but millionaires. I'm going there, and it's soon I'll be riding in my own carriage, I suppose."*

*As for the accomplishments of these girls, no list would be long enough to enumerate them, and no rash man so ungallant as to abridge them. They can cook, sing and play the piano, scrub, take care of a house and mind children, milk cows, raise chickens, weed garden beds, go to market, sew, patch and knit, make cheese and butter, pickle cucumbers and drive cattle.*

*No wonder when he heard they were coming a farmer out in Kansas wrote: "John Lee, Vice-President of the Merchantile Marine Steamship Company: Dear Sir: I am a widower with a couple of married daughters, but I want a new wife, who is to come out here to Kansas the minute the 'Baltic' gets in. There is only one other house near mine. She can tell my house by the green shutters. Tell her not to make a mistake."*

*Doing "home work" in the dreary confines of their New York tenement, an Italian immigrant family earns a precarious living by making artificial flowers.*

## *Hard Lessons for Greenhorns*

Bewildered at first by their strange new country, most immigrants huddled together in urban enclaves of their own. But once they had entered the Germantowns and Jewtowns and Little Italys, their fine new freedoms were whittled away by the sharp edge of poverty.

Each ethnic slum was a tiny world that clutched at its denizens, holding them to a few filthy streets, markets and sweatshops. Seldom did the overworked laborer or his child-burdened wife have the will to venture a couple of miles to the wonderland of theaters and department stores. Elderly residents on the upper floors of tenements hesitated to attempt the ramshackle stairs; some did not leave their dingy flats for years.

The degradation of the slumdwellers triggered angry volleys from reform-minded muckrakers. Journalist Jacob Riis, himself an immigrant from Denmark, presented grim photographs and stories of festering tenements and their disease-ridden inmates; he warned his readers that "In the battle of the slum we win or we perish. There is no middle ground." Novelist Frank Norris, reporting on the Pennsylvania coal fields, quoted a miner's opinion of the lot of local immigrants: "They don't live no better than dogs." Norris disagreed. Their existence, he said, was much worse: "They live in houses built of sheet-iron, and boards, about fifteen feet square and sunk about three feet in the ground. Of course there is but one room, and in this room the family—anywhere from six to ten humans—cooks, eats and sleeps."

Despite the long-range benefits of such exposés, the immigrants received little practical help and almost no immediate improvement in their condition. Happily, there were exceptional cases, and a few city governments took steps to make life easier for the poor. Tom L. Johnson *(overleaf)*, the benevolent mayor of Cleveland, Ohio, introduced cheap public transportation and built parks, playgrounds and public baths to help brighten the dreariness of slum life. But in most other places, immigrants were forced to rely upon themselves. Banding together to seek strength in numbers, they joined religious brotherhoods, community welfare

*Drab houses crowd a byway in Chicago's grimmest ghetto, the Maxwell Street area. This section was occupied successively by groups of Irish, Jews and Negroes.*

associations, labor unions and local political clubs.

Politically, most of the newcomers were inexperienced and naive; they spent years learning how to use the American party system to make government responsive to their needs. In the interim, many became the clients —and the victims—of machine politicians, who, although they did offer some leadership and protection, nevertheless set records for venality and greed. Perhaps the greediest of all was tough William Flinn, a Pittsburgh boss who made several fortunes in high-level graft; when Flinn died in 1924, he left an estate of more than $11 million. But even lesser ward bosses amassed millions in small "donations" from shopkeepers, criminals and companies angling for business with the city.

Thus any crafty boss had plenty of money to spend, and he spent it liberally down in the wards whence came his power. In New York City, with its immigrant-crowded slums, the casting of bread upon the waters brought manifold returns to the Tammany organization of boss Charles F. Murphy. One of Murphy's lieutenants, George W. Plunkitt, was an expert on philanthropy. "If a family is burned out," explained this rich and genial grafter, "I don't ask whether they are Republicans or Democrats. I just get quarters for them, buy clothes for them if their clothes were burned up, and fix them up till they get things runnin' again. Who can tell how many votes these fires bring me?"

Because Flinn and many other bosses were immigrants with big immigrant followings, bigoted natives held the newcomers responsible for political corruption. But the muckraking champions of the hapless immigrant put bossism and corruption in proper perspective. "The boss," said Riis, "is like measles, a distemper of a self-governing people's infancy." Lincoln Steffens, investigating municipal corruption for a series in *McClure's* magazine, discovered that New York and Chicago were well governed despite their immigrants, while Philadelphia, "the purest American community of all," was "the most hopeless." Steffens concluded: "The 'foreign element' excuse is one of the hypocritical lies that save us from the clear sight of ourselves."

The prejudice and scorn of natives drove many immigrants in upon themselves and hardened them. However, most of the younger immigrants, and almost all

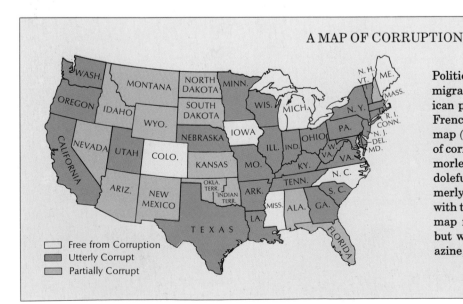

## A MAP OF CORRUPTION

Free from Corruption
Utterly Corrupt
Partially Corrupt

Political corruption, sometimes blamed on the immigrants, touched off loud explosions in the American press—and a curious echo far off in France. A French editor used wild imagination to produce a map (*left*) purporting to show accurately the degree of corruption throughout the United States. This humorless work of cartography was accompanied by a doleful prognosis for the U.S.: "The organism, formerly healthy, has become incontestably infected with the germs of contagious decay." The lugubrious map may have aroused serious concern in France, but when it was reproduced in an American magazine, readers were amused in spite of themselves.

*The poor man's champion, Mayor Tom L. Johnson of Cleveland, glows among his constituents. His municipal reforms gave Cleveland a nationwide reputation.*

of the second generation, sought to win acceptance by Americanization. They were pathetically eager to abandon Old World ways and dress, to speak English without an accent, to acquire American friends and manners. A Polish immigrant, gainfully employed in a Polish section but frustrated by the "foreign" environment, wrote a touching appeal to the Massachusetts Commission on Immigration: "I want live with american people, but where? Not in the country, because I want go in the city, free evening schools and lern. I'm looking for help. If somebody could give me another job between american people, help me live with them and lern english—and could tell me the best way how I can lern—it would be very, very good for me."

Ironically, the ideal of assimilation was responsible for the immigrant's ultimate tragedy. Some parents encouraged their children's efforts to Americanize. Others resisted with the full strength of their Old World authority. But in either case, the results were usually the same. Even before the children grew up and left home, they drifted away from the family, and the gap between the generations steadily widened.

Complete Americanization was the goal of Mary Antin, a gifted girl from Russia whose family settled in a Boston slum. With the father's encouragement, the children went their own way; Mary devoted herself to study and writing. She scored a grade-school triumph when her poem in praise of George Washington was published in the Boston *Herald*, and her father proudly distributed among friends all the papers he could buy. In the arrogance of her youthful fame, and with a faith in America that defied yet demanded explication, Mary wrote passionately, "It would have been amazing if I had stuck in the mire of the slum. By every law of my nature, I was bound to soar above it, to attain the fairer places that wait for every emancipated immigrant."

Mary Antin and countless fellow immigrants did escape from the slums into the American mainstream. But they left behind many others—people once as optimistic as they—to hopeless poverty and frustration.

*Staring blankly, a young slum woman pauses in her crude kitchen amid evidence of defeat and despair: a broken faucet, an abandoned boot, a littered floor.*

*Orville Wright makes the first airplane flight, while brother Wilbur trots alongside.*

# Flying Machines

# *A Decade of Ups and Downs*

*Aerial flight is one of that class of problems with which man can never cope.*

SIMON NEWCOMB, 1903

*Success assured. Keep quiet.*

ORVILLE WRIGHT, 1903

In the year 1903, almost nobody believed that men would ever fly. Most people simply agreed with the noted astronomer, Simon Newcomb, when he said that it was just common sense to keep both feet firmly planted on the ground.

At least two men knew better. In December 1903, on a sandspit at Kitty Hawk, North Carolina, Orville and Wilbur Wright were putting the last touches on a "whopper flying machine" they had built at their bicycle shop in Dayton, Ohio, and shipped to Kitty Hawk for tests. Confident of success, Orville sent the telegram above to his father in Dayton urging secrecy. Then quite suddenly on December 17 it was done. The two brothers piloted their flimsy, jerry-built machine on a series of wobbly flights, the longest one lasting 59 seconds and covering 852 feet.

The next day, only two newspapers across the entire United States saw fit to carry the story. Other papers were still grousing over an earlier flight attempt that seemed to confirm the national suspicion that the sky was a place only for birds, angels and fools. Just nine days before Kitty Hawk, the secretary of the Smithsonian Institution, Samuel Langley, had tried to launch

a winged contraption from the roof of a houseboat on the Potomac River in Washington, D.C. Langley, backed by a $50,000 grant from the War Department, had spent five years perfecting his machine. But while boatloads of reporters and government officials watched expectantly, the craft had left its catapult and plunged nose first *(opposite)* into the Potomac.

With the soggy demise of Langley's pioneering effort most people's interest in aviation took a nose dive. Not until 1908, after Wilbur and Orville demonstrated an improved version of their airplane to U.S. government officials, did the public awaken to the fact that men were truly flying. Then it seemed that everyone wanted to get into the air.

Across the country, inspired backyard aeronauts started building their own weird-looking contraptions, all designed to go the Wrights one better. Sportsmen and military daredevils mingled at fashionable air meets. As this whirl of airborne activity got under way, Wilbur Wright observed soberly that "the age of flight had come at last." Indeed it had, but there was still no agreement whatever *(following pages)* on the best way for man to stay aloft, now that he had finally gotten there.

*A $50,000 disaster, Samuel Langley's airplane caught a wing tip on its catapult and broke apart in mid-air before plummeting into the Potomac River.*

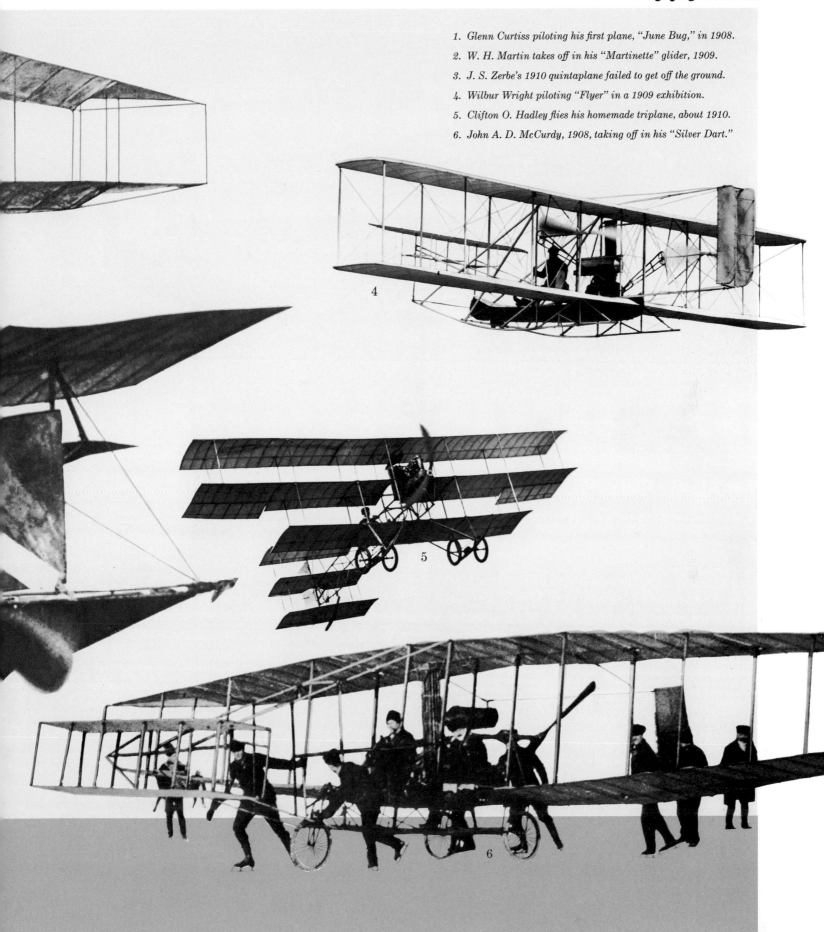

1. Glenn Curtiss piloting his first plane, "June Bug," in 1908.
2. W. H. Martin takes off in his "Martinette" glider, 1909.
3. J. S. Zerbe's 1910 quintaplane failed to get off the ground.
4. Wilbur Wright piloting "Flyer" in a 1909 exhibition.
5. Clifton O. Hadley flies his homemade triplane, about 1910.
6. John A. D. McCurdy, 1908, taking off in his "Silver Dart."

Despite its two imposing overhead rotors, this prototype helicopter hammered together by the blacksmith of Jetmore, Kansas, never made it off the town's main street.

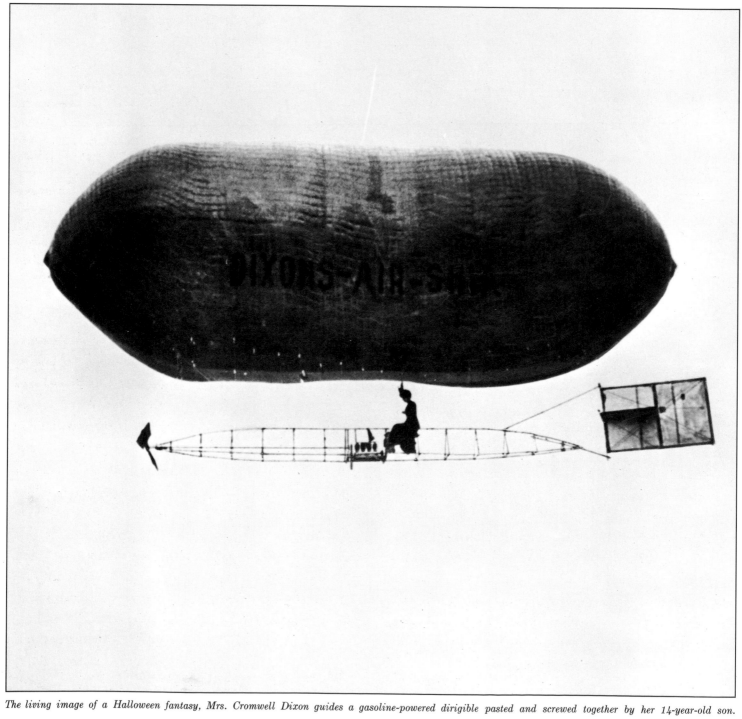

*The living image of a Halloween fantasy, Mrs. Cromwell Dixon guides a gasoline-powered dirigible pasted and screwed together by her 14-year-old son.*

CROMWELL DIXON

MRS. DIXON

## A Grand Old Gasbag

While newborn planes were staggering aloft, an even more unlikely type of aircraft began to drift across the American skies. It was called the dirigible, and it was a gas-filled, sausage-shaped balloon propelled by an engine. The most precocious of the various dirigible-builders of the decade was 14-year-old Cromwell Dixon of Columbus, Ohio. With the aid of a determined mother, Dixon designed and actually flew several airships, including one model that could be driven through the sky like a bicycle, by pedaling. In the following letter to *St. Nicholas* magazine, Dixon's proud mother describes the setbacks and successes of the youthful aeronaut.

*Dear St. Nicholas*          *Columbus, Ohio*

*As I attend to my son Cromwell's business, I will write you a few lines pertaining to his work, and also send you some very good photographs of Cromwell himself and his sky-bicycle and of his air-ship. Most people prefer the sky-bicycle, as it was the little fellow's own invention and he built it himself, even cutting the silk for the gas-bag over a pattern that Mr. Knabenshue, the great Toledo aeronaut, cut for him. I stitched it and we both worked night and day until it was finished. Then we varnished it. We had to be very careful for if we had not watched it carefully it would have stuck together so tightly that we could not have gotten it apart, but after several days it dried sufficiently to put on another coat, and so on until we had five coats. Then we kept it inflated until the last coat was dry. Cromwell was happy then, as he could get ready to test his sky-bicycle.*

*Then while at one of the Columbus parks, where Cromwell was engaged to make a flight, he lost everything he had by fire, so all had to be done over again. He went to work and made the second outfit even better than the first, so you see what a brave little man he was. Not even a sigh, when all he had accomplished lay a heap of ashes. He turned to me and said: "Well, mother, we must commence tomorrow on our new outfit so that we can fulfill our engagements this summer."*

*Cromwell has always been of a mechanical nature. Having shown his preference for such things, I encouraged him, and helped him besides. He lost his father when a baby.*

*He attended the St. Louis balloon and air-ship carnival, where Cromwell was a great favorite and where he made a beautiful flight in his sky-cycle.*

*Very truly yours,*
*Mrs. C. Dixon*

*The U.S. Army's first aircraft was this dirigible, bought in 1908. But since no one could fly it except its inventor, T. S. Baldwin (near tail), it was never used.*

A glum crew of young students endures the flag drill in a school pageant.

# The Grownups Close In

*"Penrod, what excuse have you to offer before I report your case to the principal?"*
*The word "principal" struck him in the vitals. Grand Inquisitor, Grand Khan, Sultan, Emperor, Tsar, Caesar Augustus—these are comparable.*

PENROD, BY BOOTH TARKINGTON

The first decade was a watershed in the special world of the young. In keeping with the Victorian era just past, the decade began as a time of strict rules and frequent moralizing. At home, fathers were not inclined to spare the rod, and at the dinner table children were well scrubbed and not heard. In the classroom, whispering was an offense that merited a whipping. Sunday-school teachers darkly noted that erring mortals had once been punished with Noah's flood, and that next time God planned to finish the job with fire. In harmonious chorus, antiseptic novels and schoolbooks like the pervasive McGuffey's *Readers (pages 114-117)* sang of the rewards of virtuous behavior, warning that lazy children would come to no good end.

But as soon as the class—or dinner or chores or whipping—was over, the kids nodded their heads, promising to be good, and then raced around the corner into their own private domain. There they were self-reliant, and could fashion their own brand of happiness with nothing more than a dog or a pocketknife, or a doll and some paints. Over the course of a year, games ebbed and flowed in a mystical, unspoken sequence. Kites, for example, might be popular for a week. Then kites would vanish and mumblety-peg or roller skates or kick-the-can or stilt-walking took over. Competition was often fierce and, in some games, the stakes were formidably high: if kids were playing "keepers" in marbles, a lost agate might set back the loser as much as 50 cents —more than a month's allowance.

But as the decade progressed, this rigid code and its underlying doctrine of self-reliance was no longer as necessary or as easy to uphold as it had been. Grownups moved in—for better or for worse—on the kids' world in ways they never had before. Daniel Beard, author of the wildly popular *American Boys Handy Book* (how to conduct snowball warfare, etc., *pages 110-113*), helped found the Boy Scouts in 1910. Publishing czar William Randolph Hearst made popular a new kind of kids' reading matter called the comic strip *(pages 102-105)*. Baseball cards, like those at right, were issued by cigarette companies in their packages as a sly bid for kids' attention. A collector's dream set would have 522 cards, but probably would not include the legendary shortstop Honus Wagner, whose picture had to be bootlegged by the tobacco companies since he refused to pose on grounds that he did not want to encourage youngsters to smoke.

SCHAEFER, WASHINGTON

MATHEWSON, N. Y. NAT'L

Joe Tinker
OF THE
Chicago Nationals

EVERS, CHICAGO NAT'L

CUBS

Frank L Chance
OF THE
Chicago Nationals

LAJOIE, CLEVELAND

KEELER, N. Y. AMER.

WALSH CHIC. AMER.

COBB, DETROIT

YOUNG CLEVELAND AMER.

JENNINGS, DETROIT

BENDER, PHILA. AMER.

PIRATES

Fred L Clarke
OF THE
PITTSBURG NATIONALS

M. BROWN, CHICAGO NAT'L

DELEHANTY, WASHINGTON

# *Spokesmen for Mischief*

The Sunday funnies made a colorful entrance on the American scene on October 18, 1896, when the New York *Journal* published what it termed "eight pages of iridescent polychromous effulgence that makes the rainbow look like a lead pipe." Comic strips were an instant success and became daily features. The violent humor of the first funnies (one cartoon character performed such antics as breaking the jaw of a Negro boy and laughing merrily) was tempered to accommodate protesting parents. Pranks and embarrassing blunders became staple fare in *Happy Hooligan* and *The Captain and the Kids (below and opposite)*, and happy animal drawings *(top, right)* decorated the funnies page. For the first time, kids were finding something in the newspapers that reflected their own love of deviltry. When Buster Brown and his dog Tige arrived in 1902 in a strip *(overleaf)* that idealized mischief behind a thin veil of sermonizing, kids' feelings about themselves were expressed so perfectly that thousands of boys and dogs across the nation were soon sporting the names of Buster and Tige.

HAPPY HOOLIGAN

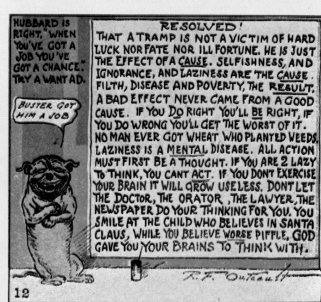

PLUCK AND LUCK
STORIES OF ADVENTURE.

No. 496.    NEW YORK, DECEMBER 4, 1907.    Price 5 Cents.

FROM BOOTBLACK TO SENATOR;
OR, BOUND TO MAKE HIS WAY. By HOWARD AUS—

No. 392    NEW YORK, JUNE 25, 1910    FIVE CENTS

BRAVE AND BOLD
WEEKLY

THE B—
or Win—

WOR—
An Interesting

No. 364.    NEW YO—

FRED FEAR—
OR, A WEE—

NEW MAGNET LIBRARY ~No. 893~
The Blind Man's
Daughter
By
NICHOLAS
CARTER

No. 43.    5 Cents
WIDE AWAKE
A COMPLETE STORY    WEEKLY    EVERY

YOUNG WIDE AWAKE'S
OR, THE NARROWEST ESCAP—
By ROBERT LENNOX

MOTOR STORIES
THRILLING ADVENTURE    MOTOR FICTION
NO. 12    FIVE
MAY 15, 1909    CENTS
MOTOR HIT'S
or CASTAWAY IN THE BAHAMAS

FRANK MERRIWELL IN DIAMOND L—
TIP TOP WEEKL—
An Ideal Publication for the American
No. 725    MARCH 5, 1910    5 C—

PLUCK AND LUCK
COMPLETE STORIES OF ADVENTURE.

No. 186.    NEW YORK, DECEMBER 25, 1901.

THE POOREST BOY IN NEW-Y—
AND HOW HE BECAME RICH.
By N. S. WOOD, THE YOUNG AMER—

There was a scream of terror from the girl, echoed by a shout from those on the—gine was rapidly approaching. Dropping the valise heavily to the platform,—the track, right in the path of the engine, and dragged the girl to—

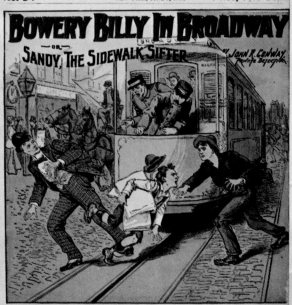

BOWERY BOY
LIBRARY
Issued Weekly. By Subscription, $2.50 per year. Entered according to Act of Congress in the year 1906, in the office of the Librarian of Congress, Washington, D. C., by THE WINNER LIBRARY CO., 165 West Fifteenth St., New York, N. Y.
No. 34    NEW YORK, JUNE 9, 1906.    Price, Five Cents

BOWERY BILLY IN BROADWAY
—OR—
SANDY, THE SIDEWALK SIFTER    By John R. Conway

Bowery Billy seized Sandy, the newsboy, in a desperate endeavor to save him from being crush—underneath the on-coming car.

WORK AND W—
An Interesting Weekly for Y—
No. 300.    NEW YORK, SEPTEMBER 2, 190—

FRED FEARNOT AND THE MON—
OR BREAKING UP A SWINDL—
By HAL STANDISH

"Here! Here! What's this?" Fred exclaimed.    "She hasn't paid back—one of the men, "and we are taking her furniture, under the co—paid it," asserted Fred, "for I gave her the money for that purp—

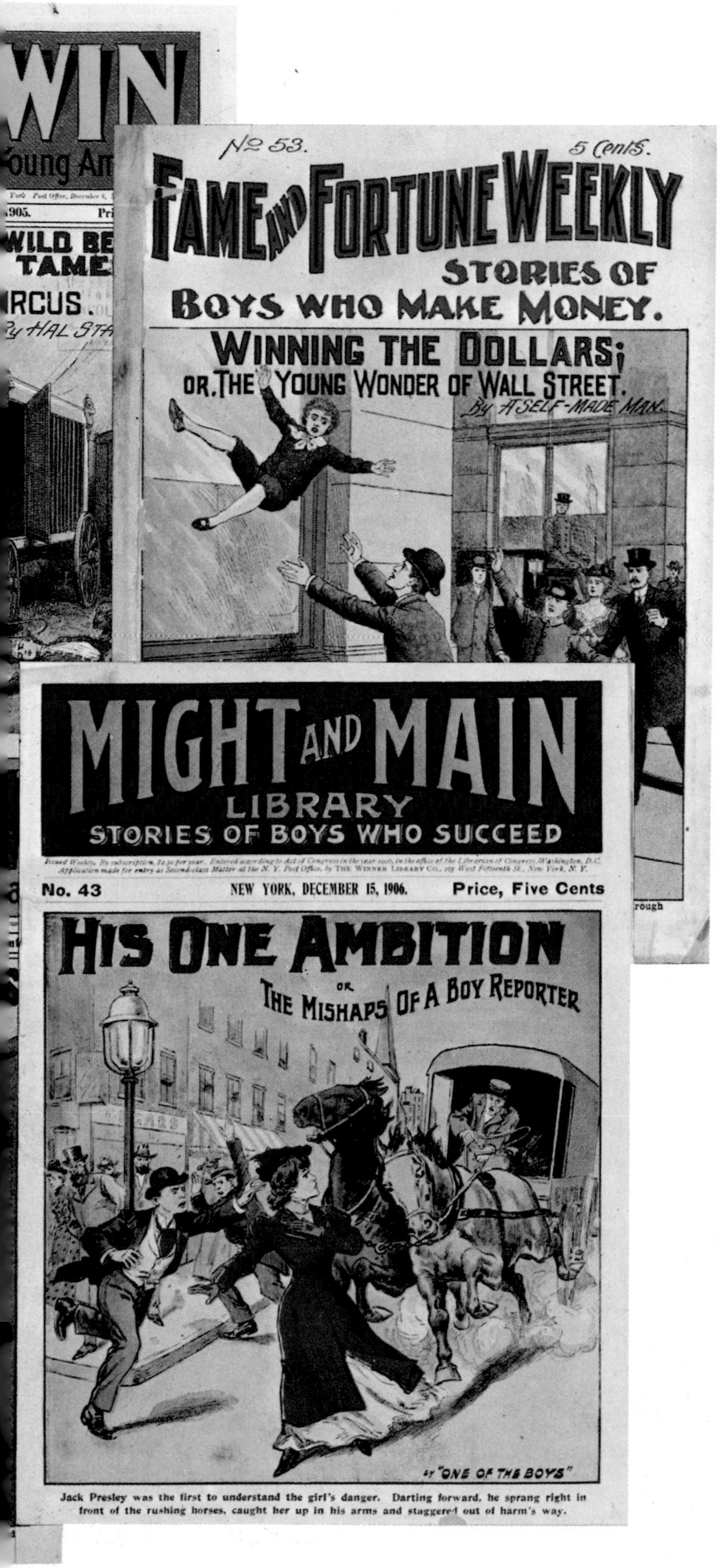

WIN
Young Am
905.      Pri
WILD BE
TAME
RCUS
By HAL STA

No 53.          5 Cents.

# Fame and Fortune Weekly
### STORIES OF
## BOYS WHO MAKE MONEY.
## WINNING THE DOLLARS;
### OR, THE YOUNG WONDER OF WALL STREET.
By A SELF-MADE MAN.

# MIGHT AND MAIN
### LIBRARY
### STORIES OF BOYS WHO SUCCEED

Issued Weekly. By subscription, $2.50 per year. Entered according to Act of Congress in the year 1906, in the office of the Librarian of Congress, Washington, D.C.
Application made for entry as Second-class Matter at the N. Y. Post Office, by THE WINNER LIBRARY CO., 165 West Fifteenth St., New York, N.Y.

No. 43          NEW YORK, DECEMBER 15, 1906.          Price, Five Cents

rough

# HIS ONE AMBITION
### OR
### THE MISHAPS OF A BOY REPORTER

BY "ONE OF THE BOYS"

Jack Presley was the first to understand the girl's danger. Darting forward, he sprang right in front of the rushing horses, caught her up in his arms and staggered out of harm's way.

Hidden behind many a geography book full of dull facts about a country called Asia or something, there lurked a suspiciously ungeographical magazine. In the classroom, at friends' houses, almost anywhere away from the disapproving eyes of adults, boys turned to their favorite form of written fantasy, the dime novel— really a long short story bound into a five- or ten-cent magazine like those shown at left. The heroes who sprang from these pages—Fred Fearnot, Nick Carter, Bowery Billy—were personfications of the American ideal: pure of heart, doggedly ambitious and brave beyond belief.

The greatest of all dime-novel heroes was Frank Merriwell (pages 108-109), created for Tip Top Weekly by George Patten, alias Burt L. Standish. Patten wrote some 20,000 words a week and reached 125 million readers, but virtue had to be its own reward, for he received a maximum of $150 per issue, and died in poverty.

His fictional creation had a far better time of it. Frank Merriwell, in fact, could do no wrong. As Patten wrote, "His handsome proportions, his graceful, muscular figure, his fine, kingly head and that look of clean manliness . . . stamped him as a fellow of lofty thoughts and ambitions." First at Fardale Academy, then at Yale College, and later during world-wide adventures, the magnetic Frank Merriwell accomplished every task with perfect ease. Time and time again, he won the day in boxing, baseball (he possessed a pitch that curved in two directions), football, hockey, lacrosse, crew, track, shooting, bicycle racing, billiards and golf. He outwitted Chinese bandits, Texas rustlers and urban thugs. In addition to his feats of brain and muscle, he was good. When classmates stole a turkey from a farmer as a prank, Frank stayed behind to pin a five-dollar bill to the roost. He loved his mother, his alma mater and his country; he abhorred poor sportsmanship, drinking and bullies. The creator of this paragon of virtue once said, "I confess that my imagination was often pumped pretty dry," but for 20 years, he turned out such thrilling episodes as the one on the following pages.

# Tip Top Weekly

An ideal publication          for the American Youth

Issued Weekly.  By Subscription $2.50 per year.  Entered as Second Class Matter at New York Post Office by STREET & SMITH, 238 William St., N. Y.

**No. 269.**                                        **Price. Five Cents.**

# FRANK MERRIWELL'S GREAT VICTORY
## OR THE EFFORT OF HIS LIFE

BY BURT L. STANDISH

FRANK LITERALLY FLUNG HIMSELF FORWARD WITH A LAST GREAT BURST OF SPEED, BREASTED THE TAPE, AND PLUNGED INTO THE ARMS OF BART HODGE.

## An Average Day for Frank

During one spring season Frank Merriwell was so busy starring on the baseball team and bidding for top place in his Yale class that he had no time for track. So he trained his friend Bart Hodge to run against Hood of Harvard in the mile event of the intercollegiate track meet. Unfortunately, Bart sprained his ankle at the very last moment, but he decided to run anyway.

*Preparations were being made for the mile run. Bart joined the starters. Then, at the last moment before the men were called to the mark, a great mad roar went up from the Yale stand. "Merriwell! Merriwell! Merriwell!"*

*Frank Merriwell was seen running across the field. "On your mark!" cried the starter. The men leaned forward on the line. "Set!" There was a straining of muscles. The runners crouched like human wolves ready for the spring.*

*Bang! Away they went. Frank Merriwell had reached the field in time to take his place as the substitute of Bart Hodge. He shot off from the mark with Dalton of Columbia at his shoulder.*

*Merriwell had counted on taking his pace from Hood, and he was disappointed when the man permitted Fealing of Georgetown and Dalton of Columbia to draw away. His disappointment increased as still others took the lead.*

*It occurred to him that Hood was playing a crafty trick. He was willing to sacrifice himself in order that Harvard might come out ahead of Yale. In order for Yale to take the lead she must win this event, while Harvard could lose it and still be at the top by a small margin.*

*At the half Frank gradually increased his speed. Old coaches looked on in consternation as they saw Frank pass man after man in that quarter. It seemed that he had made his burst too soon.*

*Now Merriwell felt the terrible strain, and he realized that Hood had used him to set the pace.*

*"Tricked!" groaned a Yale coach. "Merriwell can't keep it up to the tape!"*

*Now Hood was pressing Frank, who began to feel that he could not carry out the mighty task, yet who would not give his body the least relaxing. Every muscle of that splendid frame was tense, every nerve was strained. Frank's face was white as chalk. Once he seemed to reel. In that moment Hood reached his side and took the lead by twenty-six inches.*

*A cloudlike mist fluttered before Frank Merriwell's eyes. He knew that Hood had passed him. Through the cloud he saw grotesquely dancing figures beyond the finish. But his ears were deaf from the wild yells of the thousands.*

*"Come on, Merriwell—come on!"*

*"Hood wins!" roared the Crimson. "Har-vard! Har-vard!"*

*Frank knew the finish must be near. He gathered himself for the effort of his life. Then, just when it seemed that defeat was certain, he literally flung himself forward with a last burst of speed, passed the side of the Harvard runner, breasted the tape and plunged into the arms of Bart Hodge.*

*He had dropped, and like a mighty Niagara rose the roar that greeted the victor, for Merriwell had won at the last moment, and Yale was in the lead.*

*Roar! Roar! Roar! It went up to the blue sky! Men hugged each other, pounded each other, shrieked, danced and also died with joy.*

*"Merriwell!" roared the throng. "Merriwell! Merriwell!"*

*Set among mementos of the era, the "Handy Books" by Dan Beard and his sisters were among the most prized possessions of kids who devised their own playthings.*

# Guidebooks to the Kids' World

"I'd rather be an American boy than President of the United States, or anything else in the world," Daniel Carter Beard once said. In 1882, Beard—who, as a young man, worked at various times as an illustrator, engineer and map maker—magnificently regressed to childhood and wrote a compendium of kids' lore, *The American Boys Handy Book*. No sugary dose of adult wistfulness, the *Handy Book* described in simple terms how to build kites, snowshoes or sailboats, how to stuff birds, trap rabbits or raise frogs. Beard's sisters later wrote a similar, though less mechanical, guide for girls. For generations of youngsters, these volumes, excerpted below with illustrations on the following pages, were indispensable reference works on the real art of growing up.

### HOW TO MAKE AN ARMED WAR KITE

*These aero-nautical cutters might be appropriately named the Scorpion, "Stingerree," Wasp, or Hornet, because they fight with their tails. To win the battle you so manoeuvre your warrior that its tail sweeps across and cuts the string of your antagonist. The cutters to be attached to the tail are made of sharp pieces of broken glass called knives. Fasten three knives together with wax so that each shall point in a different direction, bind on this three slips of thin wood lengthwise to hold the wax and glass firmly, and cover neatly with cloth or kid. Boys participating in this war of kites should always bear in mind the fact that it requires but little skill to cut an unarmed kite, and that there is no honor or glory to be gained in vanquishing a foe who is unable to defend himself.*

### HOW TO MAKE A BOOMERANG

*With boiling water scald a piece of well-seasoned elm, ash or hickory plank that is free from knots. Allow the wood to remain in water until it becomes pliable enough to bend. When it has assumed the proper curve, nail on the side pieces to hold the wood in position until it is thoroughly dry; after which the side pieces may be removed, with no fear that the plank will not retain the curve imparted. Saw the wood into as many pieces as it will allow, and each piece will be a boomerang that only needs to be trimmed with a pocket knife, and scraped smooth with a piece of glass to make a finished weapon. A boomerang cast by a beginner is very dangerous in a crowd, for there is no telling where it is going to alight, and when it does come down it sometimes comes with a force enough to cut a small dog almost in two.*

### TAXIDERMY—HOW TO SKIN A BIRD

*Place the bird on its back upon the table, in such a position that the head will be toward your left hand; then, with the knife in your right hand you are ready to make the incision. With your left hand separate the feathers, left and right, from the apex of the breast bone to the tail. Cut a straight slit through the skin between these points. . . .*

### HOW TO ORGANIZE A GIRLS' CLUB

*Make out a list of the girls you intend to invite to join the club, and ask them to meet at your house. Explain your plans, and let the would-be members sign the constitution, which should previously be neatly written out in a blank book, with the name of the club, date, and the full name of the founder of the society. Later, if the club finds the constitution adopted inadequate for its needs, it may be amended to suit the society.*

### MAINTAINING YOUR BICYCLE

*The arrangement of the holes for oiling of bicycles varies with each make; but, bear in mind, wherever there is friction, oil is needed, and if you examine your wheel carefully you will find that this has been provided for. Look for oiling points on front and rear axles, crank-axle bearings, pedals, steering head, brake-lever, brake-spoon, chain at joints if oil is used on chain.*

*Sticks plus snow make a snowman*

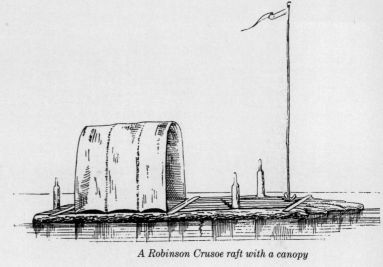

*A Robinson Crusoe raft with a canopy*

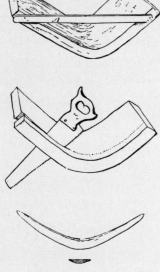

*Three stages in the making of a boomerang*

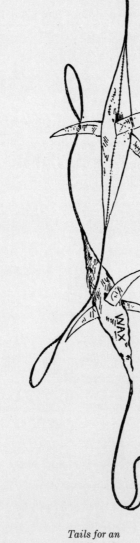

*Tails for an armed war kite*

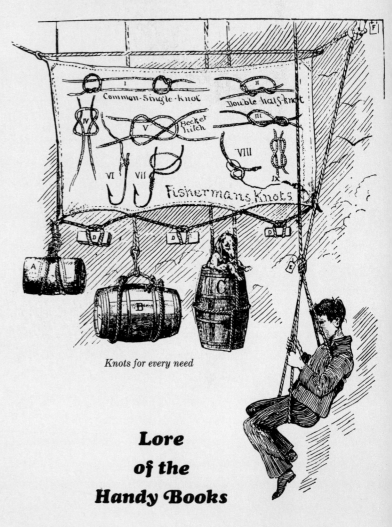

*Knots for every need*

## Lore of the Handy Books

In the true spirit of childhood, the creations of the *Handy Books* achieved a maximum of happiness with a minimum of materials. Telephones *(far left and far right)* were made of baking-powder boxes, drawing paper and string; a raft was made of logs fastened together with wooden pegs ("they will hold much more firmly than iron nails," wrote Dan Beard). The cheapest and most important ingredient of all was imagination—the kids' own.

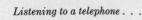

*Listening to a telephone . . .*

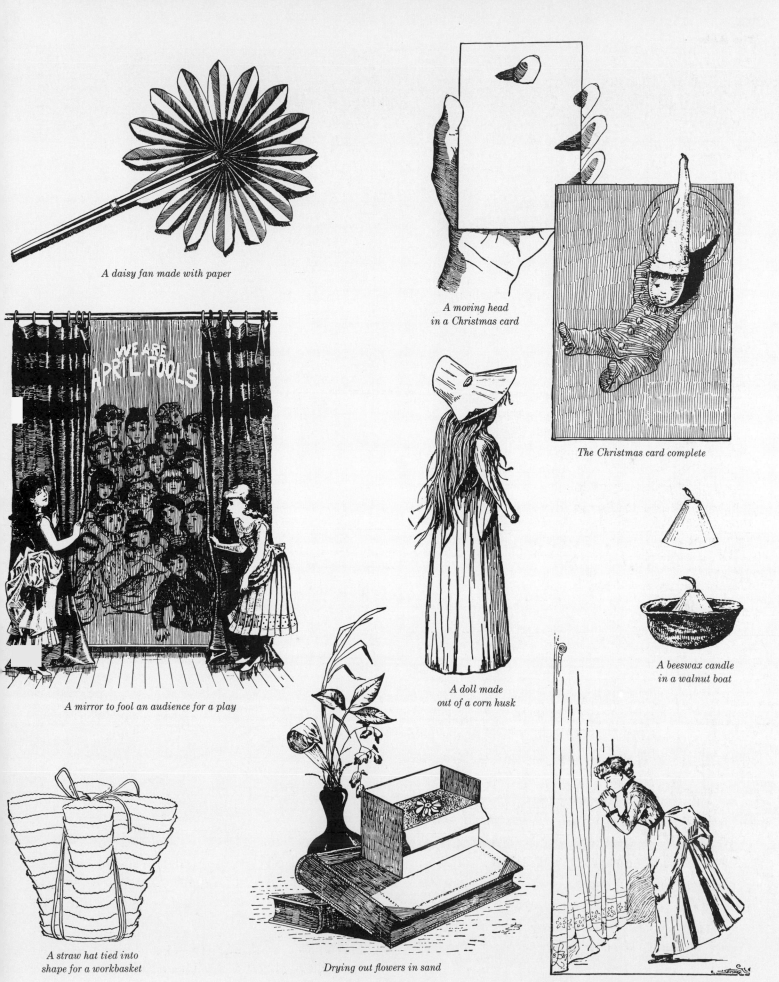

A daisy fan made with paper

A moving head
in a Christmas card

The Christmas card complete

A mirror to fool an audience for a play

A doll made
out of a corn husk

A beeswax candle
in a walnut boat

A straw hat tied into
shape for a workbasket

Drying out flowers in sand

. . . and speaking into the telephone

## Dear Old Golden Rule Days

School, that unavoidable misfortune which befell all freedom-loving kids, offered a rather somber introduction to the world of books. While in some urban schools children were beginning to learn by doing things themselves *(right)*, millions of youngsters still cut their reading teeth on a five-book series known as McGuffey's *Readers*, containing short tales *(below)*, verses, pronunciation and spelling lessons, and an anthology of English and American literature. Written in the 1830s and 1840s by a university professor named William Holmes McGuffey, they remained the literary staple for countless schools well into the 20th Century. McGuffey grew up on a farm chopped out of the Ohio wilderness, and his *Readers* were successful because in an America still predominantly rural they spoke the language of rural children.

*Charles was an honest boy, but his neighbor, Jack Pilfer, was a thief. Charles would not take anything which did not belong to him; but Jack would take whatever he could get.*

*Early one summer's morning, as Charles was going to school, he met a man who had oranges to sell. The man wished to stop and get his breakfast, and asked Charles if he would hold his horse while he went into the house.*

*But he first inquired of the landlord if he knew Charles to be an honest boy, as he would not like to trust his oranges with him, if he was not.*

*Yes, said the landlord, I have known Charles all his life, and have never known him to lie or steal; all the neighbors know him to be an honest boy, and I will engage your oranges will be as safe with him as with yourself.*

*The orange man then put the bridle into Charles' hand, and went into the house to eat his breakfast.*

*Very soon Jack Pilfer came along the road and seeing Charles holding the horse, he asked him whose horse he had*

*Youthful investigators, urged on by a rather heavy-handed message from the blackboard, tackle the Eskimo Housing Question during a 1904 geography lesson.*

there, and what was in the baskets. Charles told him that the owner of the horse was in the house, and that there were oranges in the baskets.

As soon as Jack found there were oranges in the baskets, he determined to have one, and going up to the basket, he slipped in his hand and took out one of the largest, and was making off with it.

But Charles said, Jack, you shall not steal these oranges while I have the care of them, and so you may just put that one back into the basket.

Not I, said Jack, as I am the largest, I shall do as I please; but Charles was not afraid, and taking the orange out of his hand, he threw it back into the basket.

Jack then attempted to go around to the other side and take one from the other basket; but as he stepped too near the horse's heels, he received a violent kick, which sent him sprawling to the ground.

His cries soon brought out the people from the house, and when they learned what had happened, they said that Jack was rightly served; and the orange man, taking Charles' hat, filled it with oranges, as he said he had been so faithful in guarding them, he should have all these for honesty.

QUESTIONS

1. What is this story about?
2. Which is the honest boy?
3. What kind of boy was Jack Pilfer?
4. What is the job of a landlord?
5. What kind of character did the landlord give Charles?
6. How can boys secure a good name?
7. What advantage is there in possessing a good character?

*A botany lesson, aided by a lavish display of flowers imported into the classroom, elicits rapt attention from tiny grammar-school children in Washington, D.C.*

*An oddly assorted but dutiful public-school orchestra, with a barefoot cello player in the front row, tunes up at the first schoolhouse in St. Petersburg, Florida.*

*Freed for the day by the final school bell, boys and girls clamber up ladders and through the pipework of an ingenious early playground structure in Denver.*

# The Old Hometown

*Main Street in Dorrance, Kansas, seen from the town's water tower, snakes off into prairie.*

# Life in a Prairie Town

*This town is the fruit of great aspiration, and we who live here now have a debt to posterity
that we can pay only by still achieving, still pursuing; we must learn to labor and to wait.*

WILLIAM ALLEN WHITE, EDITOR OF THE EMPORIA, KANSAS, *GAZETTE*

Patience was a way of life for at least 45 million Americans at the turn of the century. Those millions, comprising the 60 per cent of the population that resided in towns of fewer than 2,500 people, endured as country folk always had, in the grip of the seasons, following the rhythm of planting and harvesting. So it was for the wheatgrowers of Dorrance, an austere little town huddled on a windy prairie in north-central Kansas.

During its half-century of existence, Dorrance had never been more than a speck on the map, but it had seen a lot of history. The area had been crossed by Indian hunters, by wagon trains of settlers and gold seekers. In 1867, the Union Pacific Railroad tracks reached Dorrance, bringing with them the German, Irish and other immigrants who accounted for much of the town's modest growth after 1870. By 1910, when Dorrance was incorporated, it had only 281 citizens, yet it was one of the most important towns in Russell County.

Not without cause, the townspeople took quiet pride in their community. Dorrance had everything a country town really needed: a good public school, with four teachers and about 100 pupils; a bank and a hotel; four churches; a variety of stores and businesses; telephone and telegraph service. This was a progressive town. Decades ago, farmers had built windmills that still pumped their water. Recently a few men had acquired modern steam-driven threshers, and the Mahoney family even bought a car when autos were still a novelty in the cities.

The people themselves, shown here in pictures taken by Leslie Halbe, the banker's son, were exactly what their town suggested: a plain, durable folk who feared God and worked hard. In their need for relief from the prairie's raw isolation, people drew together and got on well. German and Frenchman, Catholic and Mennonite pitched in to help one another at harvest time, and to outfit the town's baseball team. No one got rich, but no one was poor.

In such small towns life had a continuity that extended beyond the grave. The dead, buried in cemeteries inside the town, were as much a part of Dorrance as the blacksmith's shop and Weber's lumberyard; their graves were visited on Decoration Day by all the citizens, led by Civil War veterans in faded uniforms. Few people, living or dead, left Dorrance; almost everyone stayed on, content and patient to labor and to wait.

*Dorrance's station crew waits for a train under a sign listing distances to the nearest big cities. Here salesmen detrained and hawked their wares for miles around.*

*Two landmarks on Main Street, the post office and village drugstore, were built of limestone from nearby quarries and lumber that had to be brought in by rail.*

Dorrance's telephone switchboard operator had few calls and plenty of time to chat. Twice, she had no work at all when blizzards knocked down all the wires.

The Citizens' State Bank issued loans to families between harvests. One major cause for seasonal borrowing was the average farmer's need for a dozen work horses.

*Under hats pegged to the wall, town workers and visitors on business are served family style by a dexterous short-order cook in Sheetz's Restaurant on Main Street.*

*Wearing their Sunday suits and straw boaters, two young farmers, Peter Steinle and Henry Heinze, share a buggy ride to Dorrance from their outlying spread.*

*The Lutheran Church lets out its congregation, about 60 families strong. Dorrance had three other denominations, all with white frame churches of their own.*

*A wheatgrower unloads his crop at a grain elevator. This elevator was constructed by German immigrants who brought with them the winter wheat grown locally.*

A farmer sets out from the local John Deere dealership with a new header machine to reap his wheat. Harvesting began around July 1 and took about 12 days.

A man identified as S. Shilts tended pigs to supplement the income from his wheat crop. A typical Dorrance farmer, he cultivated about 300 acres of prairie land.

*Helping at harvest time, a wheat farmer's family gathers together on the water wagon driven out to refill the steam engine that powered the threshing machine.*

## Big City Down River

One hundred miles to the east of Dorrance lay the bigger, more bumptious hometown of Junction City, Kansas. Thanks to its handy location at the junction of the Republican and Smoky Hill Rivers, it was a thriving business center of 5,000 citizens. And there was not one of them who was not proud of the way the town had grown: by 1900 there were a full score of restaurants. The matching complement of drug, department and food stores drew the farmers from miles around and kept the natives prosperous. At right and on the following pages is a sampling of these Junction City emporiums, together with lists of prices a shopper in the town—and thousands of other towns much like it—paid in the first decade.

### Drugstore Prices

#### SODA FOUNTAIN

| | | | |
|---|---|---|---|
| Ice Cream Soda | 10¢ | Grape Lemonade | 15¢ |
| Plain Soda | 5¢ | Orangeade | 5¢ |
| Root Beer Float | 5¢ | Lemon Phosphate | 5¢ |
| Sundae | 10¢ | Buttermilk | 5¢ |
| Cantaloupe Sundae | 15¢ | Egg Milk Chocolate | 10¢ |
| Egg Drinks | 10¢ | Coffee (iced or hot) | 10¢ |
| Tonic Water | 10¢ | Cakes | 5¢ |

#### DRUGS

| | | | |
|---|---|---|---|
| Witch Hazel | 25¢ | Corn Plasters | 10¢ |
| Aruica Salve | 10¢ | Wart Remover | 10¢ |
| Bromo Seltzer | 10¢ | Castoria | 35¢ |
| Wine of Cardui | $1.00 | St. Jacob's Oil | 25¢ |
| Cough Syrup | 25¢ | Hair Balsam | 50¢ |

*The Loeb & Hollis Drug Store, one of the best in Junction City, sold perfume, cigars and "fancy goods," and had a soda fountain, latest in drugstore fixtures.*

*Frey's New Cafe, on the main street, was open all night, and served such delicacies as oysters in season. The stairs (upper left) led to private dining rooms.*

## Dinner Menu

### APPETIZERS

| | | | |
|---|---|---|---|
| Canteloupe, half | 10¢ | Sliced Tomatoes | 10¢ |
| Sliced Orange | 10¢ | New Radishes | 5¢ |
| Young Onions | 5¢ | Sliced Cucumbers | 10¢ |

### SOUP
Old Fashioned Navy Bean, 10¢

### MAIN COURSE

| | | | |
|---|---|---|---|
| Channel Catfish | 20¢ | Chicken Fricassee | 20¢ |
| Pork Tenderloins | 20¢ | Roast Beef | 15¢ |
| Omelet with Jelly | 15¢ | Pork and Beans | 15¢ |
| Roast Pork, Apple Sauce | 20¢ | Boston Baked Beans | 10¢ |

### VEGETABLES

| | | | |
|---|---|---|---|
| Corn on the Cob | 10¢ | Pickled Beets | 5¢ |
| Buttered Beets | 5¢ | Cold Slaw | 5¢ |
| Mashed Potatoes | 5¢ | Salad | 10¢ |

### DESSERT

| | | | |
|---|---|---|---|
| Lemon Layer Cake | 5¢ | Raspberries and Cream | 10¢ |
| Ice Cream | 10¢ | Rhubarb Pie | 5¢ |
| Ice Cream and Cake | 15¢ | Green Apple Pie | 5¢ |

### BEVERAGES

| | | | |
|---|---|---|---|
| Coffee | 5¢ | Tea | 5¢ |
| Milk | 5¢ | Buttermilk | 5¢ |

*Aproned butchers at the Park Meat Market, named for its parkside location, stand ready to cut a customer's meats to order. Wild game was a shop specialty.*

### Meat and Poultry Prices

| | | | | | | | |
|---|---|---|---|---|---|---|---|
| Spring Chicken | 7¢ lb. | Roosters | 15¢ ea. | Turkey | 10¢ lb. | Veal | 10¢ lb. |
| Beef | 10¢ lb. | Hens | 7¢ lb. | Duck | 6¢ lb. | Breakfast Bacon | 12½¢ lb. |
| Sausage | 12½¢ lb. | Pork | 10¢ lb. | Duck, Dressed | 10¢ lb. | Goose | 5¢ lb. |

## Grocery Prices

### PRODUCE AND DAIRY PRODUCTS

| | | | |
|---|---|---|---|
| Red Apples | 30¢ pk. | Dried Apricots | 10¢ lb. |
| Seed Potatoes | 35¢ bu. | Dried Prunes | 5¢ lb. |
| Onion Sets | 3 qt. 25¢ | Eggs | 12¢ doz. |
| Oranges | 20¢ doz. | Butter | 18¢ lb. |
| Lemons | 15¢ doz. | Swiss Cheese | 25¢ lb. |

### HOUSEWARES

| | | | |
|---|---|---|---|
| Scrub Brush | 15¢ | Starch | 10¢ |
| Lye | 5¢ | Toilet Soap | 3 for 15¢ |
| Garden Seed | 2 for 5¢ | Candles | 1 Box 15¢ |

### CANNED GOODS

| | | | |
|---|---|---|---|
| Golden Cream Corn | 10¢ | Boston Baked Beans | 10¢ |
| String Beans | 10¢ | Oysters | 20¢ |
| Tomatoes | 20¢ | Jams | 10¢ |
| Early June Peas | 10¢ | Green Turtle Meat | $2.75 |
| Sliced Peaches | 25¢ | Sardines in Oil | 5¢ |

### STAPLES

| | | | |
|---|---|---|---|
| Tea | 40¢ | Sugar | 100 lbs. $5.80 |
| Coffee | 15¢ lb. | Salt | 100 lbs. 20¢ |
| Cocoa | 25¢ | Salad Dressing | 25¢ |
| Macaroni | 10¢ | Baking Powder | 10¢ |
| Hominy Grits | 10¢ | Gelatine | 15¢ |

*Latham's Grocery had staples (in bins, left), canned goods and produce. The wood stove, which provided the store's only heat, and a coffee mill stand at the rear.*

## Department Store Prices

### LADIES' WEAR

| | | | |
|---|---|---|---|
| Tailor-made Suit | $10.00 | Waist | $3.00 |
| Skirt | $4.00 | Corset | 40¢ |
| Chemise | 50¢ | Shawl | 50¢ |
| Bracelet | 35¢ | Silk Petticoat | $5.00 |
| Shoes | $1.50 | Bead Purse | 59¢ |

### MEN'S WEAR

| | | | |
|---|---|---|---|
| Fancy Suit | $9.00 | Coat and Vest | $7.00 |
| Trousers | $1.25 | Linen Collar | 25¢ |
| Shirts | 50¢ | Hat | $2.00 |
| Woolen hose | 15¢ | Underwear | 50¢ |
| Suspenders | 25¢ | Work Shoes | $1.25 |

### HOUSE FURNISHINGS

| | | | |
|---|---|---|---|
| Blanket | 35¢ | Wallpaper | roll 5¢ |
| Carpet | 12¢ yd. | 42-Piece Dinner Set | $2.95 |
| Hammock | $3.50 | Sheet, Double Bed | 58¢ |

### DRESS GOODS

| | | | |
|---|---|---|---|
| Gingham | 12½¢ yd. | Sewing Machine | $12.00 |
| Madras Cloth | 10¢ yd. | Embroidery | 8¢ |
| Taffeta | 85¢ yd. | Silk | 50¢ yd. |
| Calico | 6¢ yd. | Sewing Pattern | 10¢ |
| Pins | box 5¢ | Damask | 40¢ yd |

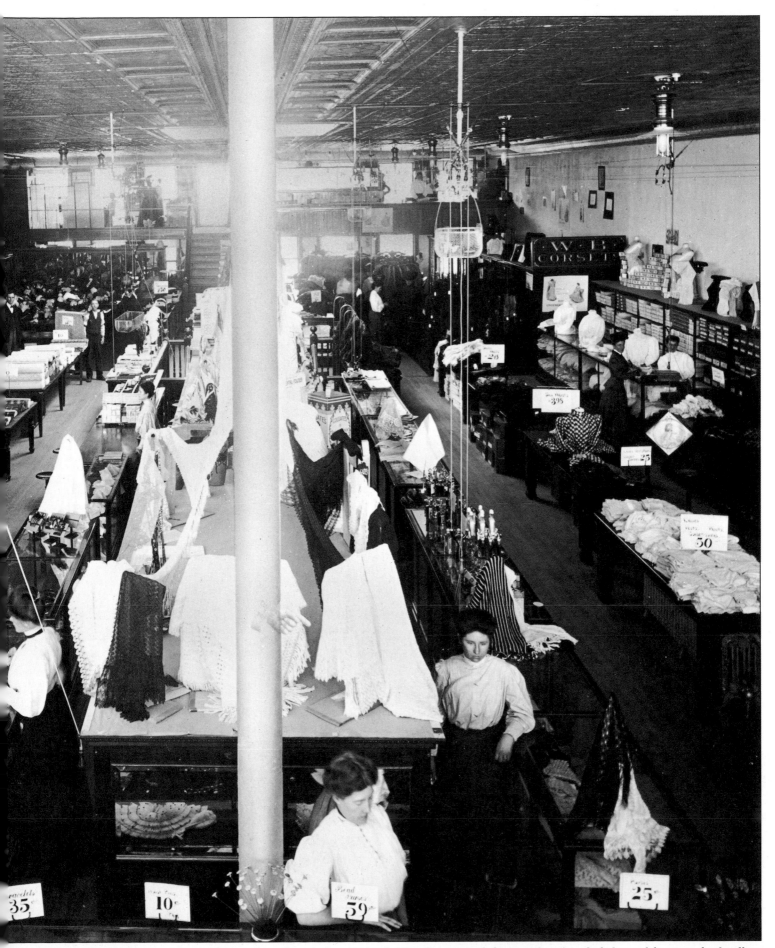

*The Pegues, Wright Department Store sold dry goods on the main floor. Baskets holding the customers' change and receipts clacked to and fro on overhead trolleys.*

## An American Family Album

*Us on the porch*

In 1900 the hometown folks had a new toy to play with—the Kodak Brownie camera, which suddenly made its appearance at the modest price of one dollar. All a person had to do was snap the shutter, and there were Mama, Papa and the kids—at home, on vacation or in school—in stiff but familiar poses that were pasted in photo albums all over America.

The pictures on these pages were made by just such amateur portraitists. The snapshot above is of the Shaw family of Eau Claire, Wisconsin. The widow of George Shaw, a lumber baron, sits at the left in

the back. Next to her is her son George Jr., then in high school; to the right stands his aunt, Mrs. Eugene Shaw. Margaret Shaw, Eugene's daughter, sits in front; the boy beside her and the young lady behind him are family friends.

The pictures at right and on the following pages were taken by kindred amateurs. Resurrected from dusty attics and library shelves—some with the subjects' names long forgotten but many with the original captions intact—they make up a homely portrait of the early years of the century.

*Sunday afternoon*

*Here we are in a lumberyard*

*Making Thanksgiving pies*

*At Uncle Herman's house*

The Campbells are coming

The Campbells are going

Fishing for a compliment

Four on a melon

*The big play*

*Speaking of buoys*

## Vacation Frolics

Summer was a time for outdoor frolics, and for just lazing around. The whole family might go to a shore resort, like the Campbells of Michigan *(upper right, on buoy, and opposite page)*, or to a camp in the woods, like the Wooldridges of Arizona *(above)*. A daughter home from school might treat her classmates to a fortnight's house party, like Esther Eva Strauss, who is eating watermelon with a cluster of school chums *(left)*.

House-party entertainment, like summer capers generally, was homemade. The girls' gentlemen callers would come from miles around, riding horseback or driving their fanciest rigs—buggies and phaetons. They amused themselves at tennis on the lawn, hayrides on wagons, teas by the riverbank or deep in the woods; at chestnut-roasting and marshmallow-toasting; at fishing from a pier, like the hatted girl on the opposite page. Wherever they went and however they passed the time, the Brownie camera went along to chronicle the fun.

*Making merry on the Chippewa*

*Four little maids from school are we*

*Whew—passed calculus*

## Off to College

For understandable reasons, family albums had a notable shortage of pictures of students laboring over their books—drudgery being a highly unmemorable experience. But the antics and comradeship of college days received plenty of attention. Who could forget the day when the girls at Beloit College gave a party in the dormitory, or the time they poked their heads through a sheet *(top right)* to pose as Bluebeard's hapless wives? And remember the night after

*You'll never take us alive!*

*Life is a cinch*

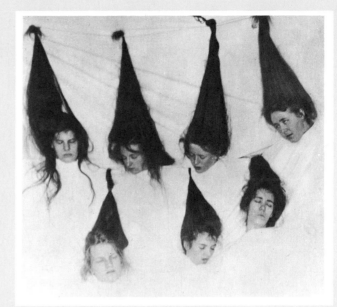

*Bluebeard's wives*

final exams *(right)*—or even the morning after the night before *(left)*—when the awful threat of the dean's ax had finally been erased? These and other pieces of nostalgic trivia found their way into family picture collections, to be pulled out years later and chuckled over by the subjects, or roundly hooted at by irreverent spouses. And the children, while wondering how their parents could act so undignified, decided that maybe the old folks had not been so hopelessly stodgy after all.

*The passing of exams—in March's room*

*The hungry bunch*

*Gate swingers*

*It's all bluff*

*"Catch anything, Miss?"*

*All aboard*

*Why the old gray mare is tired*

*Looks comfy*

## The Moods of Love

The box Brownie was a sensitive recorder of small moments to be remembered. Perhaps because the person who took the picture usually was a friend or a relative, courting couples found it easy to share the spirit of the moment with the camera. And those were moments that could not be allowed to fade, unrecorded, into the past. There was Horace Rhoads on a California pier *(far left)*, holding a parasol for the girl who became his wife. There, in a goofy hat *(above left)*, was a Midwestern Romeo grinning at a friend; and four youngsters *(left)* sitting in mock formality in another hammock. Clowning, flirting, chatting or kissing, lovers in all the little moods of courtship were shown in the family album.

*Underneath the bough*

A girls' basketball squad, evidence of the more active life women found in the new century, poses for the team picture.

The Ladies

## ❦ A Woman's Place ❦

*In other countries you may be gently urged for an appreciation of the architecture of galleries; but the American man will, in nine cases out of ten, make his first question of the visiting foreigner—"Well, what do you think of our women?"*

KATHERINE G. BUSBEY, 1910

When George Bernard Shaw was asked his opinion of American women in 1907, he answered: "Every American woman explains that she is an absolute exception and is not like any other American woman. But they are all exactly the same. The only thing to be said for them is they are usually very well dressed and extraordinarily good looking." That was exactly the way American men wanted their women: beautiful, but not so bright and sassy that they wandered from their place in the home.

The emancipation of women from male domination—as well as from fanciful costumes requiring steel-reinforced corsets (*right*) and a life close to the hearth—was barely beginning as the century dawned. Fully one quarter of the states then in the Union denied a wife the right to own property; one third of them allowed her no claim on her own earnings—even if she worked to support a shiftless husband. And 36 of them, or four fifths, denied her an equal share in the guardianship of her children.

Peons the women may have seemed, but powerless they were not. Despite their lack of legal rights, they had many a compensation. "They haven't th' right to vote," conceded Mr. Dooley, the fictitious philosopher created by humorist Finley Peter Dunne, "but they have th' priv'lege iv controllin' th' man ye ilicit. They haven't th' right to make laws, but they have th' priv'lege iv breakin' thim, which is betther. They haven't the right iv a fair thrile be a jury iv their peers; but they have th' priv'lege iv an unfair thrile be a jury iv their admirin' infeeryors. If I cud fly d'ye think I'd want to walk?"

Most women, as Mr. Dooley suggested, chose to "fly." They got their way exactly as they were expected to, by dazzling their menfolk with feminine wiles. In this course they were abetted by a flood of "women's literature"—romantic fiction that created an ideal of the softly genteel but indomitable female, and magazines that gave them practical how-to instructions for achieving the ideal. Articles preached decorum and cautioned against dangerous new ideas. *Vogue* warned in 1900, "All decent people are agreed that the emancipated novelists are not fit reading," and listed as taboo the "cancerous literature" of Ibsen, Zola and Shaw among others. Along with such admonitions went a steady stream of advice on beauty and fashion, which, as the acid Shaw noted, was American woman's most obvious asset.

To squeeze ladies into shape, manufacturers offered corsets like these.

1. *Toque with satin bow, advertised as suitable for morning*

2. *Tailored toque with velvet brim, silk crown and bow*

3. *Evening hat in flowered silk and plaited chiffon*

4. *Afternoon hat with egret plume and satin-faced brim*

5. *Evening hat in velvet and silk, made "for a blonde"*

6. *Picture hat in two-toned velvet and chiffon*

4                           5                           6

The ladies adorned themselves with clothes of great variety and elegance, and they spent an unparalleled amount of money doing it: over a billion dollars a year, $14 million of it on corsets alone. The crowning glory of every lady's get-up was her hat, and nary a woman set foot outdoors without one. It was always liberally garnished with poufs of lace, yards of ribbon, bouquets of flowers, bunches of fruit—and besides any or all of these, it frequently carried a nest of birds.

So prodigal was the slaughter of birds to appease the gods of women's fashion that at a single monthly auction in London in 1900 the plumage of more than 24,000 egrets was up for sale—a fact that the Audubon Society protested in vain. In 1905 the Sears, Roebuck catalogue devoted most of a page to some 75 versions of ostrich feathers for women's headgear; and if ostriches were not to the lady's taste, she could adorn her hats instead with clusters of purple grackles or red-winged blackbirds, ori-

oles or skylarks, pigeons or doves, thrushes or wrens—in short, with almost anything that once had chirped.

Below her fancy bonnets the lady wore equally elaborate dresses like those *(next page)* that were illustrated in 1906 in a magazine with the classy Frenchified title of *L'Art de la Mode and le Charme United*. Generally she made them herself—or had a dressmaker fashion them for her—from McCall or Butterick patterns; but mass-manufactured clothes were coming on the market as immigrant Jewish tailors poured in from pogrom-ridden Poland and Russia. "There is no place in the world where such dainty machine-made garments of all sorts can be found as in American department stores," said Katherine G. Busbey, the lady quoted earlier. The American innovation of well-made ready-to-wear clothes was accompanied by a notable native contribution to fashion: the shirtwaist, a blouse meant to be worn with a skirt. Paris couture looked down its nose on this aberration, but American women paid no heed. They took to the shirtwaist first in the 1890s. By 1905 the Sears, Roebuck catalogue was offering 150 different versions of it, from a plain one in lawn at 39 cents to a grand concoction in taffeta at $6.95. In 1907 came the peek-a-boo shirtwaist, a daring creation of eyelet embroidery that allowed the flesh of a lady's arms to show. By 1910 the national production of shirtwaists was big business; New York alone turned out 60 million dollars' worth.

The skirts with which the ladies wore their waists were generally long, but once in a while they rakishly bared an ankle. In 1905 Sears, Roebuck, never a firm to be in the vanguard, offered "Ladies' Walking Skirts"— garments that "are made expressly for convenience and are also known as the Health Skirt."

Shirtwaists and shorter skirts were more than fashion whims. Simpler clothing, easier to wear and more suitable to an active life, was demanded by the new and freer role that women had begun to seek. In increasing numbers they were going out into the world, taking jobs in offices, shops and factories. The feminist movement, agitating vigorously for legal rights, swept many women into political activity. But public life and outside work were adventures for only a daring minority. The average woman concerned herself with a traditional role—obliging her husband, rearing her children, making her nest a cozy place, easing her cares with light reading. The woman's place was still in the home.

1. *Princess gown in green chiffon velvet pressed to look like ribbing*

2. *Eton suit in blue broadcloth trimmed with folds of matching velvet*

3. *Evening gown of peach satin trimmed with lace and velvet ribbon*

4. *Indoor dress in London smoke cloth with embroidered silk braid*

5. *Gown of primrose faille, with white satin collar, cuffs; black satin revers*

# THE LADIES' HOME JOURNAL

## ROMANCE NUMBER

*With his sinuous hands on her satin flesh, a lover gives his lady—and the stay-at-home with her magazine—a glimpse of the good life.*

## The Rosy World of Romance

Just as every American man knew at the turn of the century that with hard work he was bound to get ahead, so every woman took it on faith that love conquered all. If life failed to bear her out, there was a reassuring flood of romantic fiction from magazines whose saccharine covers *(left)*—with stories to match—kept the ladies' eyes fixed on a world beyond the workaday kitchen.

The following passage is condensed from a serial in *The Delineator*. The story, like others of its kind was full of mini-tragedies. But the sensitive reader may be assured that in the final installment the dashing suitor will return to save the heroine from a life without love.

*It was all over with her past; her brief passionate love dream was forever put aside! Never a word had come from Stelvio since the witching night on the Grand Canal in Venice.*

*Now back at home in Virginia she wandered like a soul in pain, and finally one evening stole out to an old favorite spot of childhood, a hillock in the nearby forest massed with wild blossoms from Spring to Autumn. Here Margot dropped upon a bench, and for the last time, so she told herself, lived over the hour in Far Niente garden when she gave her heart away never to be recalled. She would soon be McPhail's wife, since to him her poor family must look for support.*

*Stelvio! Oh! for a last word with him to ease her bursting heart. One look only!*

*And here, through the thick underwood came to her, in answer to this cry of the heart, Stelvio in person, pale, haggard, worn, deep love and reproach in his eyes!*

*"You? You here?" she cried. "Oh! it can't be!"*

*Then his words came in an impetuous, fiery stream.*

*"I am here because I heard you were soon to marry. When Countess Fleury told me this was so I went away from home and sailed directly for America. Margot, I cannot bear it; I can't lose you; I can't let that vulgar brute take from me all my treasures. If I did not believe you love me, me only, if you can look me in the eyes and say you don't, why I will give up and go away, crushed and beaten. But I won't do it*

*without trying to keep you. That night I sang to you in Venice, I knew my voice went straight to your heart and when no word came, when silence fell between us like a black veil, I was sore and wounded, but had no thought of change."*

*"And you supposed you've had all the sorrow?" cried she, hotly. "You make nothing of my suffering."*

*She tried to withdraw the rash admission, startled by the rapture in his face, but could not, for Stelvio's arms were around her, he was kissing her face and hair.*

*"Ah! Don't struggle, Margot dearest, don't put me away, when your words, your eyes, everything, confess your love for me," he cried. "Speak! Answer me! Tell me that you are mine, mine, mine!"*

*For one brief moment she had answered his heartbeats with her own and exultingly let him hold her close. Yet she was enabled to stand firm by the promptings of her spirit.*

*"Margot, forgive me. I am a brute to torture you. God knows if I could save you from this fate without thought of myself and my own longing for you, I'd do so--"*

*"You can't, you can't," she exclaimed mournfully. "But we were happy, weren't we?" she went on, plaintively.*

*He understood her. All his being thrilled in answer to these sweet avowals, but he made no move to approach her.*

*She stood gazing after him until he struck into the highroad. Then she could see him no more for bitter, blinding tears.*

*Every young lady dreamed of a proper wedding. Even so, she could laugh at herself and at courtship's*

THE PROPOSAL

DRESSING THE BRIDE

"WITH THIS RING I THEE WED"

CONGRATULATIONS

*shenanigans, looking at stereoscopic slides like these. They came packaged in sets, captions included.*

THE WEDDING MARCH

THE BRIDE

"TO THE HEALTH OF THE BRIDE"

ALONE AT LAST

## *Another View of Love*

The ladies were of two minds about love and men. Though they palpitated over the amorous embraces that filled their romantic fiction, they held strait-laced notions about proper conduct in the presence of real live men. Women's magazines reflected this duality; the same periodicals that devoted page after page to pas-sion-filled novels ran unabashedly bluenosed articles of advice concerning the behavior of young women who had not attained the blessed estate of matrimony. The excerpt below was condensed from an article written by one Alice Preston in the *Ladies' Home Journal* for March 1908, entitled "A Girl's Preparation for Marriage."

*If I had my way every girl should be taught from her early teens that some day, in the natural course of events, Love must come to her. She should be taught that it is her fate, and a very glorious fate. On top of this she should be taught that all her days are, consciously or unconsciously, a preparation for it. She should be told that no gift, no happening of youth is comparable to this of the coming of Love; because, when Love comes, it brings in its hands the keys to a Paradise which she could nowise else nor without Love's aid enter.*

*If we are ignorant how are we to learn? First, by wishing to know things as they are, and by being willing to accept them as they are. First of all, to get a little at this matter of ig-norance as to the big bodily truths—the sacred physical facts. I do not wish to go over them, nor to go into any discussion of the truths of sex. I want merely to tell you that I believe they should be known as simply and directly as any of the other big, simple facts of life. A gardener toils in his garden, side by side with the infinite powers of life and growth, and we delight in and wonder at this partnership of the human with the divine. A man like Luther Burbank interests a na-tion. A man like Thomas Edison works night and day with the big forces of Nature, and we stand aside with respect and admiration as he goes past. And yet the poorest, most humble man and woman who become the father and mother of noble and worthy human beings are dealing with a power greater than any of these; are sharers in a mightier work, are la-boring with more marvelous forces. You may read of electrical inventions, of scientific experiments, of marvels of discovery, with wonder; men may lift their hats to Burbank and Edi-son. I confess that I rise up more awed at the sight of a noble-faced woman great with child.*

GIRLS SHOULD KNOW THE BIG, SIMPLE TRUTHS OF LIFE
*I am not making a plea for the promiscuous reading of sex lit-erature. I know girls who have, with the best intent, no doubt, gone in headlong for the sex question, have pored over volumes only suited to a well-prepared, cool, science-steadied mind—to the mind of a medical student or physician; volumes which, far from being good for these girls, put an undue weight on the subject, making it a matter of morbid thinking.*

*Too much analytic sex reading and sex thinking is one of the surest ways of breaking down even the strongest nerves, as any physician will tell you. This is why so many of the French novels dealing morbidly with such questions are con-sidered unwholesome.*

IGNORANCE CAUSES LOW STANDARDS
*Generally it is ignorance that causes all of the low standards, and almost all of the unloveliness. How, then, shall I say ear-nestly enough the things to be said, and how shall I make you see what girlhood, the glory of it, means?*

*The other day I heard a hot discussion between a young and modern girl and her middle-aged and old-fashioned aunt. The aunt had discovered that "Joan's" friend "Rebecca"—a* girl of "Joan's" own age—saw no harm in allowing a boy to hold her hand—in giving him the engagement's privileges. The aunt not only rose and shone with indignation—she fairly glittered with it. The end was that "Joan" went to her room in disgrace, her cheeks flaming with indignation. By-and-by we talked things over.

"See here," I said, "I don't think your aunt was fair. It is true, I think pretty much as she does. I mean I was always taught from the time I was a little thing to look with dismay on this sort of thing that 'Rebecca' seems to think is all right. I suppose I would as soon have let a boy hold my hand as I would myself have picked up a rattlesnake. I think I got it into my head very early from Ruskin and other sources that girls are Queens, and I one in particular over my own domain. I always made it a great point never to fail of queenly dignity—that, at least, was easy. So though I have known friendship with lots of men, also (and I say it with royal gratitude) the love of some, no one of them would any more have presumed to take the slightest liberty than a courtier would with a Queen.

### SHE DID NOT KNOW: NO ONE EVER TOLD HER

"The trouble is, most older people lay down the law, and never explain why the law was made—that this sort of familiarity that your aunt condemns so hotly acts directly and subtly on the nerves of the body, renders them morbidly sensitive, rouses the emotions and passions which it is physically harmful to have roused and played upon; that it wakens and stimulates feelings and instincts and desires that should not be wakened. A girl is not told that, by allowing these liberties that she thinks so little and harmless, her nerves and forces and powers are almost certain to become diseased, and her strength undermined. Yet these are simple and direct and serious enough facts, Heaven knows!—that every girl has the right to know."

By the time I got this far "Joan" was no longer indignant, only earnest and interested. "I did not know," she said very simply; "no one ever told me."

### A GIRL'S STANDARDS AFFECT HER MAN FRIENDS

A girl I know, who holds the most lovely and womanly and reverential relationship to every man she knows, said to me one day, when I spoke to her in admiration of it: "Oh, you see, it is easy to be the finest kind of friend to them if you just keep in mind their mothers! It seems to me I can always see their mothers back of them, following me with anxious eyes, hoping with such pathetic eagerness that only the best may come to these sons of theirs, only the best women, only the best experiences. And that makes me just as noble as I know how to be, and if I were in doubt as to my place in any man's life I should make myself face squarely this one question: 'If you were his mother would you be glad at every point to have a girl act toward him just as you are acting?'" This is, I think, a very pattern and outline of girlish power and justice and reverence and loveliness.

### THE CROWN AND CITADEL OF LOVE

None of us can quite define what Love is; but this we know—that its crown and citadel is the human body. To keep healthy hours, to think sound thoughts, breathe pure air, to dress with loveliness, to strive to be a type of warm, chaste girlishness—these are all of them a preparation for Love's coming.

I wonder if some of you think I have laid far too much stress on the importance and sanctity of the body. Well, I do not think it is possible for us to do so. Next month I want to tell you how I think we can as girls prepare our minds and spirits the more fully and worthily for the coming of Love.

*The real heroine of the first decade lived not in romantic fiction but in the American kitchen (above); and she, too, had her hero—it was Sears, Roebuck & Co.*

# A House from the Wish Book

For most young American ladies, the rosy dreams implanted by romantic reading faded as they grew up. After they married, they almost inevitably found themselves confined to the home, but to a home that was changing rapidly. Even in the country, where the majority of Americans still lived in pioneer simplicity, the women were acquiring labor-saving devices for their kitchens, fancy gewgaws for their parlors, and sometimes well-equipped boudoirs for themselves. They were able to do so largely because of a convenient new way of buying the things they had read about in their mag-

azines and books. Now they could order practically whatever they wanted out of a mail-order catalogue, no matter how far they might live from the tantalizing stores of a big city.

The merchandising idea that helped to revolutionize the American home was conceived by Aaron Montgomery Ward in 1872, but Richard W. Sears, a onetime railroad clerk later known as the "Barnum of merchandising," and A. C. Roebuck, a watchmaker, perfected it. Their modest jewelry shop, founded in 1887, became a wondrous emporium that supplied housewives from

WOOD-BURNING STOVE  $17.48

BREAD TOASTER  20¢

ICE CREAM FREEZER  $1.26

SNAP-ON HANDLE & 3 IRONS  75¢

CHERRY STONER  70¢

WOODEN ICE BOX  $8.92

COFFEE GRINDER  49¢

ENAMELED TEAPOT  58¢

## The Ladies

Maine to California with every conceivable kind of merchandise, from kitchen gadgets like "The Perfect Cherry Stoner" *(previous page)* to Sunday-go-to-meeting clothes, from farm machinery to parlor ornaments, from patent nostrums to toys for the children.

The catalogue—much of whose early copy was written by the folksy Sears himself—was fondly known to American women and their families as the "wish book." Such was its influence that a clergyman once sent Sears this unsolicited note: "A little child in one of my church schools was asked the other day, What was the Tenth Commandment? The reply was, 'Thou shalt not covet.' When asked what covet meant, she replied, 'Not to want other folks' things, but to get Sears, Roebuck catalogue and buy for yourself.'"

From the first, the catalogue pushed improvements for the kitchen. It offered marvelously fancy stoves with embossed nickel trimmings, iceboxes that made possible the safe storage of perishables, and an ice-cream freezer that was "miles in advance of any other make" and could turn out the "smoothest and most deliciously mellow cream you ever tasted." Catering to the eye as well as the stomach, Sears advertised not merely pots, but such fancy items as "The Celebrated True Blue Enameled Steel Ware Teapot" *(previous page)*, which "surpasses anything heretofore offered in fancy enameled ware, when taking beauty, strength and finish into consideration."

Sears' parlor fittings *(below)* reflected the lady's cultural aspirations. Hardly a parlor was complete without at least one musical instrument—a piano, an organ, a banjo or a guitar. In 1905 Sears devoted the astonishing total of 60 pages of its catalogue to musical instruments —double the space allotted to kitchen stoves. The Beckwith Parlor Gem Organ, with its solid oak case, was guaranteed to make "the sweetest music of any organ" for miles around, or your money back.

Among their parlor items, Sears and his staff were particularly proud of their selection of portieres, advertising a particular item as the "handiwork of one of our own artists." Indeed, they thought that one sure to be among "the handsomest portieres that you have ever been able to look at." For an added fillip the lady could buy a "Fine Imported Palm Plant," which Sears assured her was one of the kind that were "extensively used for ornamenting parlors and halls." The mail-order price did not include the large pot in which it was pictured but Sears was careful to explain that the plants "are easily set up."

ROCKING CHAIR $2.95

ROPE PORTIERE $3.98

36-IN. PALM PLANT 59¢

GRANDFATHER'S CLOCK $31.50

OAK EXTENSION TABLE $13.95

ORGAN $37.35

*Even a remote farmhouse might boast a parlor as well equipped as this one. Organ, curtains and growing plants could all be ordered from Sears' wish book.*

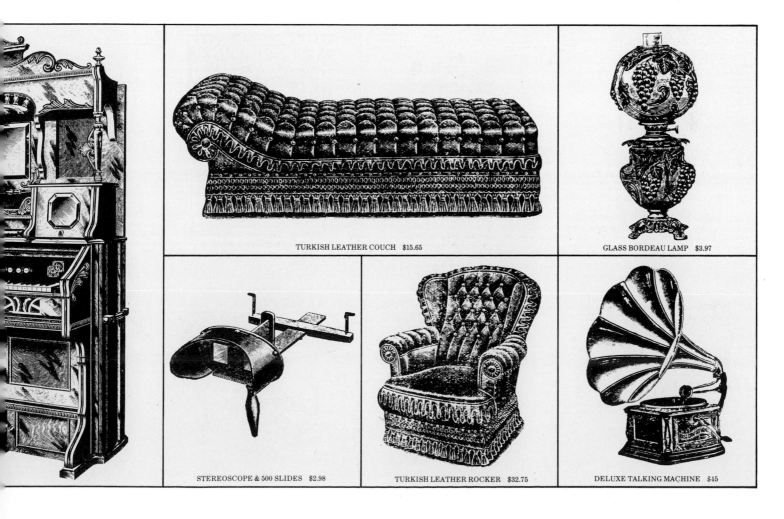

TURKISH LEATHER COUCH  $15.65

GLASS BORDEAU LAMP  $3.97

STEREOSCOPE & 500 SLIDES  $2.98

TURKISH LEATHER ROCKER  $32.75

DELUXE TALKING MACHINE  $45

*A lady's bedroom was both a boudoir and a workroom. Pins and vials graced the dresser near a writing desk (left); a sewing kit joined bibelots on shelves (right).*

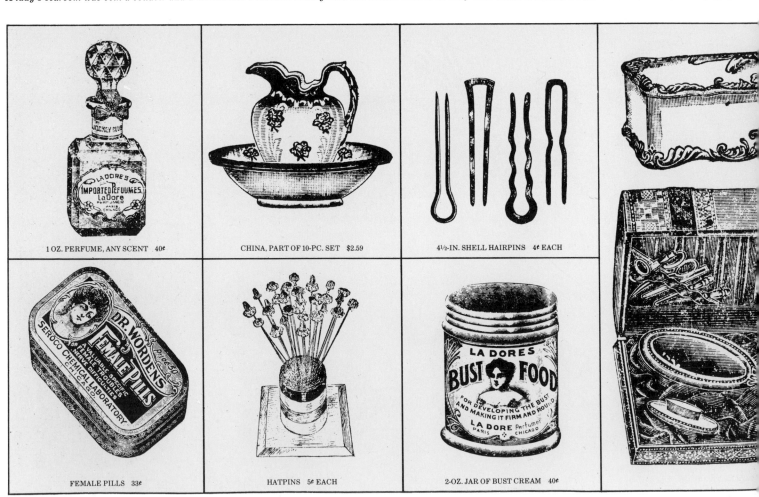

1 OZ. PERFUME, ANY SCENT  40¢

CHINA, PART OF 10-PC. SET  $2.59

4½-IN. SHELL HAIRPINS  4¢ EACH

FEMALE PILLS  33¢

HATPINS  5¢ EACH

2-OZ. JAR OF BUST CREAM  40¢

For the lady's boudoir, Sears offered, along with such beauty aids as combs, perfumes and curling irons, a pharmacopeia of patent medicines. They were dubious remedies, but they were often the only recourse of country folk in an era when illness might well be catastrophic, doctors were scarce, and pharmacology was an ill-developed science. But many customers took to the potions for another reason—the most common ingredient of nostrums was alcohol, which made them attractive to many a thirsty patient. It was the golden age of patent medicine—sales reached a high of $80 million a year—and Sears, Roebuck was not a company to overlook a good thing.

One questionable concoction among the Sears offerings was Dr. Worden's Female Pills, which contained, the catalogue advised its feminine readers, "a combination of ingredients well known for their value and effectiveness." Among these was something exotically designated Extract of Squaw Vine, which suggested to many a suffering lady that if the stuff was known to the Indians it must be magic. "In a number of cases," Sears added, "a systematic treatment with Dr. Worden's Female Pills will bring the help that can be offered."

Though Sears was alert to the dangers of quackery and warned its customers to "be careful of the medicines and treatments offered by various irresponsible companies," it unblushingly touted a product it dubbed the "world famous La Dore's Bust Food." Do you "regret that your form is not what you would like it to be"? Here was "a bust food unrivaled for its purity, perfume, elegance and effect. It is unsurpassed for developing the bust, arms and neck, making a plump, full, rounded bosom, perfect neck and arms, a smooth skin, which before was scrawny, flat and flabby."

In the winter of 1904-1905 the traffic in worthless nostrums came under heavy fire when the redoubtable Edward Bok, formidable editor of the influential *Ladies' Home Journal*, ran a series of exposés in his magazine. *Collier's Weekly* followed the next winter, and Congress came to the public's rescue by passing the Pure Food and Drugs Act, which required that drugs meet certain standards and advertising rid itself of spurious claims. Honest firms quickly fell in line, and by 1909 the Sears catalogue carried nothing more potent than epsom salts and aspirin in its drug department. An era of naïveté and simplicity was coming to a close, and Sears, whose wish book had helped to bring the outside world into the American home, was speeding the process.

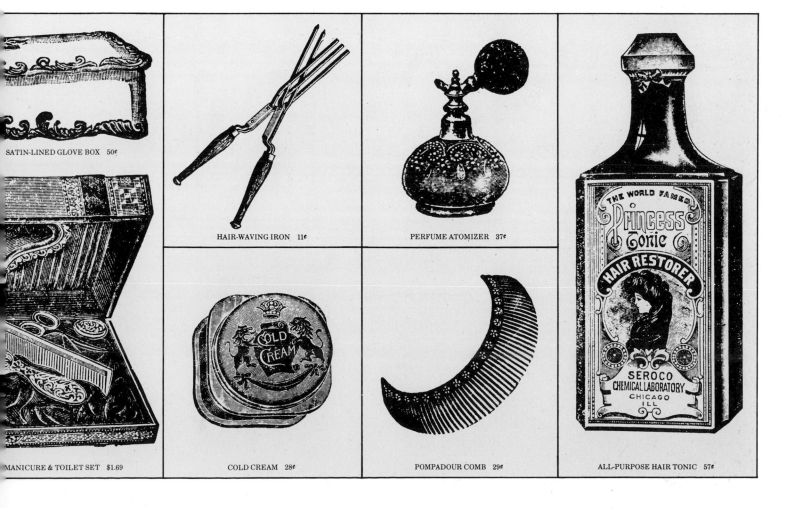

SATIN-LINED GLOVE BOX 50¢

MANICURE & TOILET SET $1.69

HAIR-WAVING IRON 11¢

COLD CREAM 28¢

PERFUME ATOMIZER 37¢

POMPADOUR COMB 29¢

ALL-PURPOSE HAIR TONIC 57¢

*Ladies of Black River Falls, Wisconsin, meet for gossip. As proper homemakers, they are drinking tea—not cocktails—and they have brought along their sewing.*

*Four "lady typewriters" take the air and flirt with the boys at lunchtime. In most offices working girls were permitted only 15 to 30 minutes for midday larks.*

*A young lady named Marcella beams with pride in her job away from home—bookkeeping at the Standard Lime & Stone Co. in Fond du Lac, Wisconsin.*

## The Ladies Leave Home

Though most women were content to play the traditional role of keeper of the home, a growing band of determined rebels was leading a march away from the pots and pans and into the exciting, man-filled world beyond. They quickly made themselves indispensable to industry and a force to be reckoned with in public affairs. At first blush the men seemed to think this invasion of male precincts was dreadful. "Men want a girl," huffed *Independent* magazine in April 1901, "who has not rubbed off the peach blossom of innocence by exposure to a rough world." Whether or not the men professed to like the new role of the ladies, the truth was that the men needed them.

In business offices, the bursting growth of the American economy had created an avalanche of paper work. A wonderful contraption called the typewriter had been invented to speed letter writing. However, male clerks found the machine a bore to operate and refused to have any truck with it. Then women tried the new machine, and from the first it was obvious that women and typewriters had been made for each other. Whereas in 1870 there had been but seven women stenographers in all of America, by 1900 there were over 100,000 "lady typewriters."

The attractions of a business job were more than simply money—though that was no small consideration, since in an office a girl could make $10 or more a week, twice what she could earn in a kitchen or an old-fashioned sweatshop. There was another, perhaps more compelling lure for the single girl—and practically every working woman was single. She found in business a world full of eager men to flirt with, a happy prospect, even if some turned out to be mashers like the plug-uglies portrayed in self-defense manuals *(next page)*.

*A threatened woman wields her bumbershoot against a masher. Here she is deftly "Stopping a blow aimed at the face."*

*Reinforced by a sprinkling of solemn male auxiliaries, the Royal Neighbors of America line up in their Kansas clubhouse for a display of uniforms, spears and banners.*

*Swinging the umbrella up, she jabs the ruffian's jaw. Alternatively, she finishes him off with a well-aimed kick to the knee.*

The working girl was not the only woman who was itching to get out of the house. Her married sister was ready, too. And with no end of handy gadgets from Sears' wish book to speed her kitchen chores, she had more time to get around than her mother had had. The first thing she usually did was join a woman's club, one of those earnest organizations dedicated to helping the poor—or simply to providing for the "self-improvement" of the members themselves.

By the end of the decade, almost a million ladies belonged to such groups. They pressured local governments to create juvenile courts, and they brought about enlightened child-labor laws. What they did most, however, was simply make the ladies feel busy and worthwhile. As the movement continued to grow, its box score of actual achievements sank so low that Edward Bok, the powerful editor of the *Ladies' Home Journal*, fired off a blast *(condensed below)* in his January 1910 issue.

---

*Now what has the average woman's club done during the past five years? What has the average woman's club done for clearer understanding of self-sex and life in the mind of the child? Absolutely nothing. What has the average woman's club done to agitate or prevent the needless blindness of 33 per cent of little blind babies? What has been done by the average woman's club toward the curse that is the one direct cause of sending 80 per cent of the women of today to the operating table? What has the average woman's club done toward the abolishment of the public drinking cup? What has the average woman's club done toward the repression in newspapers of indecent advertisements relating to private diseases, nostrums, dangerous "beauty" remedies for the skin and hair?*

*Until the woman's club shall show a more intelligent conception of its trusteeship, I insist that the woman's club up to date has been "weighed in the balance and found wanting."*

---

# Woman of the Decade

Though the ladies of the first decade may have held differing views on the proper role of the American woman, they had before them a living example of the girl they would all have liked to be. She was Alice Roosevelt, daughter of Teddy—who was himself the man of the decade. Alice Roosevelt was 17 when her father entered the White House in late 1901, and before he left he confessed *(below)* to the immensity of the role he was

*I can do one of two things. I can be President of the United States, or I can control Alice. I cannot possibly do both.*

THEODORE ROOSEVELT

asked to play. An exceptionally pretty girl, Alice was the living embodiment *(right)* of the Gibson girl, an artist's idealized concept of American womanhood. She was, moreover, every bit as spirited as her father. The newspapers delighted in calling her "a chip off the old block," and T.R. did not mind at all. With obvious relish he told a friend that Alice "does not stay in the house and fold her hands and do nothing."

Far from it. The *Journal des Débats* in Paris noted that in 15 months Alice Roosevelt had attended 407 dinners, 350 balls and 300 parties. She danced till dawn, "with the men who had least reason to expect the honor," observed one interested newsman, "and laughingly disappointed those who had counted on her."

All America was in love with her. Women named their babies Alice and dressed themselves up in Alice-blue gowns. Bands at horse races, rallies and railroad stations greeted the President's daughter with a song played in her honor, "Alice, Where Art Thou?"

Everywhere she went, she airily flouted the stodgy conventions of the decade. She smoked openly—when well-bred ladies seldom smoked even in private. On shipboard she once jumped into a swimming pool fully dressed—and drew a Congressman in behind her. In Washington she gave many a politician a run for his money at the poker table. In New York, when she found a party flagging at her Auntie Bye's, she fired a

toy pistol into the air. In Hawaii she danced the hula—an exercise thought so immodest that American tourists were normally entertained with an expurgated version.

If she startled society, Alice Roosevelt enchanted the rest of America with the unabashed pleasure she took both in herself and in the perquisites of First Family rank. She exulted in the gifts that foreign dignitaries showered on her—among them a little black dog from the Empress of China and a diamond bracelet from the Kaiser of Germany. "I was filled with greedy delight at getting them," she later wrote. And if she defied convention, she accepted the trivia of public life as gracefully as she did the lagniappe. Once at a reception in San Francisco, someone said solicitously: "You must be tired to death shaking hands with so many people." "Tired?" Alice exclaimed. "Why, I could throw my arms around their necks and kiss them."

Europe hung on her doings as breathlessly as did America. The French magazine *Femina* ran her picture on the front page, together with pictures of Europe's eligible princes. The British government considered conferring royal status upon her (a proposal her father declined) so that she might attend the coronation of King Edward VII in Westminster Abbey without violating protocol. The Japanese lined the streets and shouted *Banzai!* when she visited Tokyo. The Empress of China invited Alice to spend a night at the Imperial Palace in Peking. And the Sultan of Sulu, a Muslim who was four feet tall, was reported to have asked for the hand of the "American princess," whom he thought to add to his harem as Wife Number Seven.

Like all good princesses, Alice was indeed married, though not to the Sultan of Sulu. In the fall of 1905 she announced her engagement to an Ohio Congressman, Nicholas Longworth, whom the Washington *Times* called "the national bridegroom." Her wedding, of course, was the smash of the season, the perfect climax to a brilliant adventure in American girlship that not even the most poised and stunning of Charles Dana Gibson's imaginary ladies *(following pages)* ever truly matched.

*The image of the Gibson girl—from the tilt of her pompadoured head to the fall of her filmy skirt—Alice Roosevelt sat for a photo when she lived in the White House.*

*The ideal American girl as seen by her creator, magazine illustrator Charles Dana Gibson, was chic, haughty, graceful and above all else, shatteringly pretty.*

# The Gibson Girl

From 1890 until the First World War, American women between 15 and 30 yearned to be like the dazzling visions that floated through the ink drawings of Charles Dana Gibson. The Gibson girl—tall and stately, superbly dressed, artful but never truly wicked—first appeared in illustrations in the old humor magazine *Life*. Overnight she became the idol and the model for a generation.

"Before Gibson synthetized his ideal woman, the American girl was vague, nondescript, inchoate," wrote a reporter in the New York *World*. "As soon as the world saw Gibson's ideal it bowed down in adoration, saying: 'Lo, at last the typical American girl.'" And a European commentator exclaimed of the Gibson girl: "Parents in the United States are no better than elsewhere, but their daughters! Divinely tall, brows like Juno, lovely heads poised on throats Aphrodite might envy."

The adulation paid his pen-and-ink ladies astonished Gibson, who regarded himself as a social and political satirist, not as a style-setter for women. "If I hadn't seen it in the papers," he said, "I should never have known that there was such a thing as a Gibson girl."

He was, apparently, the only one in such ignorance. So eagerly did women look to his paragon for arbitrament in fashion that Gibson was charged with competing against the famous Butterick dress patterns, and one contemporary observer wrote: "You can always tell when a girl is taking the Gibson Cure by the way she fixes her hair."

Men were just as smitten with the Gibson girl; imitating the handsome swains who always attended her, they shaved their mustaches and padded the shoulders of their jackets. And more than one gay blade decorated his living quarters with Gibson girl wallpaper, which the manufacturer touted as just the thing for a bachelor apartment.

Gibson amiably granted licenses to put his girls on china plates, silverware, dresser sets, pillows, whiskbroom holders and virtually any other respectable surface that would accommodate them. But when an automobile manufacturer asked him to enter an advertising contest, offering a cash prize if he won but demanding the right to keep the drawing if he lost, he retorted: "I am running a competition for automobiles. Kindly submit one of yours. If acceptable, it wins an award. If rejected, it becomes my property."

Gibson used an abundance of this kind of waspish wit, together with his talent for drawing unsurpassable girls, to poke fun at the foibles of society—in fiction illustrations, in cartoons and in serialized picture stories that the artist captioned himself. Perhaps the favorite of the Gibson girl *aficionados* were the serials, such as the one on the following pages, which is taken from *Life*, in which it ran from October 1900 to July 1901.

*The eye of Charles Dana Gibson reflects the wit that sparked his drawings.*

THE WIDOW AND HER FRIENDS, by Charles Dana Gibson

*1. SHE CONTEMPLATES THE CLOISTER*

*2. SHE DECIDES TO DIE IN SPITE OF DR. BOTTLES*

3. SHE FINDS THAT EXERCISE DOES NOT IMPROVE HER SPIRITS

4. SHE FINDS SOME CONSOLATION IN HER MIRROR

5. SOME THINK SHE HAS REMAINED IN RETIREMENT T

*6. SHE IS THE SUBJECT OF SOME HOSTILE CRITICISM*

*7. SHE LOOKS FOR RELIEF AMONG SOME OLD FRIENDS*

*8. SHE GOES INTO COLORS*

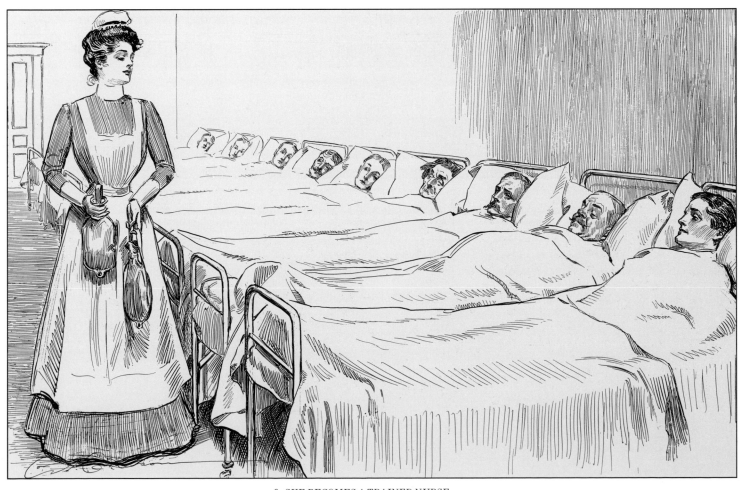

*9. SHE BECOMES A TRAINED NURSE*

*10. SHE GOES TO THE FANCY DRESS BALL AS "JULIET"*

*11. SHE IS DISTRESSED BY A VISION WHICH APPEARS TO BE HERSELF*

*12. AND HERE, WINNING NEW FRIENDS, NOT LOSING THE OLD ONES, WE LEAVE HER*

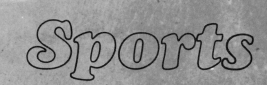

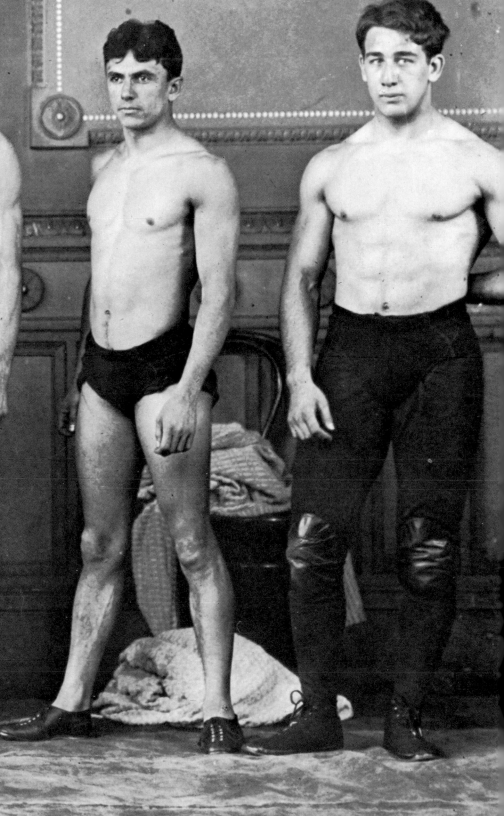

The New York Athletic Club wrestling squad lines up for a show of muscle.

# Brave Deeds by Some Bully Boys

*In life, as in a football game, the principle to follow is: hit the line hard; don't foul and don't shirk, but hit the line hard!*

THEODORE ROOSEVELT

It was a bully time in American sport. Boxing fans flocked by the tens of thousands to witness fights such as the widely trumpeted "Battle of the Century" *(pages 200-201)* between the incomparable Jim Jeffries and the skillful Negro Jack Johnson, who beat white fighters and charmed white girls with equal ease.

Baseball had truly gone big league with the formation of a second major league called the American to rival the long-established National. Now small boys had twice the number of heroes to root for: Honus Wagner and Willie ("Hit 'em Where They Ain't") Keeler were joined by new idols like Chief Bender, the full-blooded Indian pitcher for the Philadelphia Athletics, and Tyrus Raymond Cobb, fiery center fielder of the Detroit Tigers.

Amateur sport had also gone big time with a rush. The first Olympics had come to the United States *(pages 198-199)*. College football, until recently a muddy sort of grunt-and-push amusement confined to a few Eastern colleges, had begun to blossom as a rival even to baseball. Chunky Willie Heston led the 1901-1904 Michigan squads of Coach Fielding H. ("Hurry-up") Yost to such an awesome string of high-scoring victories that Michigan became known as the "point-a-minute"

football team. Carlisle Indian School, a tiny school for Indians in Pennsylvania, fell heir to a remarkable athlete named Jim Thorpe, who single-handedly demolished such great powers as Army and Penn. Yet in this decade the premier football teams were still those of Harvard and Yale, whose gentleman halfbacks hit the line with a savagery that others found hard to match.

It was not that others did not try. By 1905 college and high-school football had become so ferocious that 19 players were killed during the season. President Theodore Roosevelt, despite his vigorous exhortations about the virtues of bashing headlong into the line, persuaded a group of college presidents to draw up a more humane code of rules. The result of the White House meeting was a newer, more open type of game which Yale and Harvard, naturally, mastered in a trice. Undefeated through the seasons of '05, '06 and its first nine games of '07, Yale met a Harvard team that in the latter season had also not tasted defeat. But Yale, sparked by the slashing runs of its halfbacks—and a new play called the forward pass, which completely baffled the foe —swept to a 12-0 victory in a game that Old Blues would swear was the finest athletic contest in history.

*Lowering his tousled head, Yale's sophomore halfback Stephen Philbin prances through a confusion of Harvard tacklers in a championship game of 1907.*

# *Nasty Surprise for the Nationals*

When a sportswriter named Byron Bancroft Johnson put together the American League in 1900, the tradition-bound, tight-fisted leaders of the 24-year-old National League saw no threat to their hold on the game. But after three years of tense interleague warfare, in which the upstart Americans lured away fans and players, the Nationals gave up and sued for peace. On March 6, 1903, a code of Joint Playing Rules was signed and became the baseball law of the land. Better yet, from the fans' point of view, six months later the Boston Amer-icans, champions of the new league, signed a contract to meet the National-League-leading Pittsburgh team in a postseason series for the baseball championship of the world. The first World Series began on October 1 in Boston's Huntington Avenue grounds. The Americans quickly showed themselves equal to the challenge, polishing off the five-out-of-nine series in the eighth game. At right are two condensations from the prideful Boston *Post*, reporting the highlights of the crowd's interference in the third game, and the victory of the eighth.

*Swarming eagerly over the ball-park fence in Boston, part of the record crowd of 25,000 scrambles for a free look at the chaotic third game of the first World Series.*

*O*ctober 4, 1903— It was the greatest day in attendance the Boston Americans have ever known, more than 18,000 of the 25,000 being paid attendance. Swarming into the field, the eager thousands put ball playing temporarily out of the question. Finally Patrolman Louis Brown of Station 10 appeared with a long section of rubber hose. Using it partly as a rope, partly as a club, the police gradually drove back the human wall. Members of both nines were using their bats in much the same manner till finally the diamond and a mimic outfield had been cleared. Right here was where Boston lost the game before it was ever started. A ground rule was made whereby a hit into the crowd would be good for two bases. Before the third inning had been completed the visitors made four base hits, three of which should have been easy outs. The two runs resulting were the margin by which the home team lost.

October 14, 1903— Boston's American League team defeated Pittsburgh at the Huntington Avenue grounds yesterday and thereby won the world's championship. It was the eighth and decisive game, Boston winning five to Pittsburgh's three. Big Bill Dineen shut the National League team out without a run. Hardly had the mighty Wagner closed the ninth inning with a third futile swing at Dineen's elusive curves when a wild yell of triumph went up. The Boston Americans had vindicated the confidence of their supporters most nobly. While the grandstand swayed and rocked with the mighty salvos of applause, while Boston's players were borne by the fans in triumph to the dressing room, a dozen grey-clad Pittsburgh players, alone and almost unnoticed, walked slowly across the field and headed for the distant gate. Fallen champions they were, who had at last met their Waterloo in Boston.

*Pittsburgh's National League champions glumly watch their Series loss. Fourth from the left is Honus Wagner, the Pirate star who struck out to end the series.*

*The tug-of-war (above), in which the stalwarts of the New York Athletic Club finished fourth, was the decisive event of the first Olympic Games held in the U.S.*

## Olympian Confusion in St. Louis

The Third Olympic Games, held as an adjunct to the St. Louis World's Fair of 1904, were more notable for their giddy confusion than for athletic virtuosity. Only six foreign countries showed up. As a result, the U.S. won 22 of the 23 track and field events. And the Games became a dogfight among the various athletic clubs that had sponsored the American competitors.

It also became a kind of athletic freak show. In a bizarre competition called Anthropology Days, a leaden footed American Indian won the 100-meter dash in 11.8 seconds with an African Pygmy scuttling along in the rear at 14.6. And an Ainu from Japan threw the 56-pound hammer one yard and a few odd inches. That was the low point until Fred Lorz, apparent winner of the marathon, received his crown from none other than Alice Roosevelt—and had it unceremoniously snatched away when a local truck driver confessed he had given Lorz a lift over the last part of the course.

The final indignity occurred when the New York Athletic Club eked out a second in the hammer throw and a fourth in the tug-of-war *(above)*, to score an overall Olympic victory—whereupon the second-place Chicago A.C. protested. That was too much for the St. Louis *Post-Dispatch*, and it roasted the loser in the editorial excerpted at right.

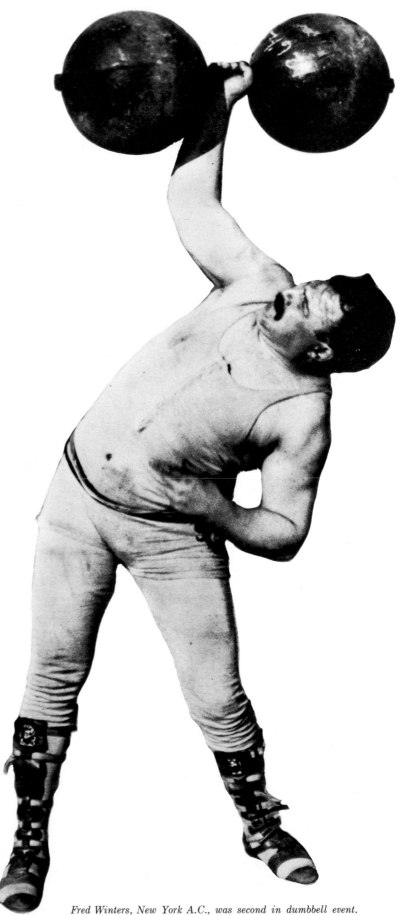

While 19,000 spectators were on their feet and cheering, the Chicago Athletic Association was protesting the four points by which the New York Athletic Club defeated them for the Olympic championship. The three points for John De Witt's second in the hammer throw were protested and the one point for fourth in the tug-of-war also was. The method of protest makes clear the underlying motive. The Chicago men were fairly beaten and to the undying shame of the Western country, a western organization has shown that it does not know how to take a beating.

*Fred Winters, New York A.C., was second in dumbbell event.*

# "The Negro Showed No Yellow"

On July 4, 1910, Jim Jeffries came out of retirement to try to wrest the heavyweight boxing championship from Jack Johnson, the first Negro to hold that title. Bigoted Americans cheered for the defeat of the black swash- buckler who clearly did not know his place. Jack London —novelist and devout racist—recorded for the San Francisco *Chronicle*, with the headline above and story condensed below, the country's surprise at the outcome.

JACK LONDON

*Johnson has sent down to defeat the chosen representative of the white race, and this time the greatest of them all. And, as of old, it was play for Johnson. From the opening to the closing round he never ceased his witty sallies, his exchange of repartee with his opponent's seconds and with the spectators. And, for that matter, Johnson had a funny thing or two to say to Jeffries in every round. The golden smile was as much in evidence as ever, and neither did it freeze on his face nor did it vanish.*

*Johnson played, as usual, blocking and defending in masterly fashion. And he played and fought a white man, in a white man's country before a white man's crowd. And the crowd was a Jeffries crowd. When Jeffries sent in that awful rip of his the crowd would madly applaud, believing it had gone home to Johnson's stomach, and Johnson, deftly interposing his elbow, would smile in irony at the spectators, play-acting, making believe he thought the applause was for him—and never believing it at all.*

## GREAT BATTLE A MONOLOGUE

*The greatest battle of the century was a monologue delivered to twenty thousand spectators by a smiling Negro who was never in doubt and who was never serious for more than a mo-*

*ment at a time. Never once was he extended. No blow Jeff ever landed hurt his dusky opponent. Johnson came out of the great fight practically undamaged. The blood on his lip was from a recent cut received in training, which Jeff managed to reopen.*

*While Jeff was dead game to the end, he was not so badly punished. What he failed to bring into the ring with him was his stamina, which he lost somewhere in the last seven years. His old-time vim and endurance were not there. As I have said, Jeff was not badly damaged. Every day boys take worse beatings in boxing bouts than Jeff took today.*

*Jeff today disposed of one question. He could not come back. Johnson, in turn, answered another question. He has not the yellow streak. But he only answered that question for today. The ferocity of the hairy-chested caveman and grizzly giant combined did not intimidate the cool-headed Negro. Many thousands in the audience expected this intimidation and were correspondingly disappointed. Johnson was not scared, let it be said here and beyond the shadow of any doubt. Not for a second did he show the flicker of a fear at the Goliath against him.*

## QUESTION OF THE YELLOW STREAK

*But the question of the yellow streak is not answered for all time. Just as Johnson has never been extended, so has he never shown the yellow streak. Just as a man may rise up, heaven knows where, who will extend Johnson, just so may that man bring out the yellow streak, and then, again, he may not.*

*Jabbing, hooking, Johnson kept up a banter with ringsiders and taunted the floundering Jeffries during the fight: "Mister Jeff, you ain't showed me nothin' yet."*

*A Charles Dana Gibson cartoon satirizes the social treadmill of the wealthy*

# Heyday of the Big Spenders

*We are not rich. We have only a few million.*

MRS. STUYVESANT FISH

Mrs. Stuyvesant Fish, long a leader of high society, had good cause to lament the meagerness of her fortune. At one opulent party, as she and Mr. Fish arose to depart early, a vulgar parvenu named Harry Lehr said arrogantly, "Sit down, Fishes, you're not rich enough to leave first."

To the dismay of the Fishes and other refined old families, they had lost pre-eminence to two generations of prodigiously wealthy Johnny-come-latelies. These raw provincial millionaires could not be denied admission into capital-S Society, the inner circle of glittering people who wintered in Palm Beach, summered in Newport or Bar Harbor, and visited London and Paris as casually as they dined at Delmonico's. Society was being democratized with alarming speed.

Indeed, money alone now made Society go round—and at a hectic whirl. The Very Rich, armed with more cash than they had time to use, spent it competitively, to impress and to outdo one another. They shelled out millions for pompous mansions *(next page)* and huge steam yachts, and for indigent noblemen to wed their daughters. They kept dozens of servants, horses and autos. In fact, it was said of one member of New York's fabulous Belmont clan that he kept "everything but the Ten Commandments."

Spicy accounts in the press of upper-crust shenanigans delighted gossip-column readers; the *pièces de résistance* for plutocrat-watchers were the parties of the Very Rich, especially their masked balls. To these spectacular functions the elite came by the giddy hundreds, wearing costumes that cost as much as $5,000 each. The hit of one ball was a small millionaire and his large wife, who came dressed up as a French king and a Norman peasant. Everybody roared when a malapropian footman announced them to the guests as "Henry the Fourth and an enormous pheasant."

The shocking costs of such parties—$100,000 and up—troubled the conspicuously consuming rich less than the social complications involved in staging one. Even the most adroit hostess stretched her skills to mount a proper ball, coordinating the extra servants, wines, and perhaps a complete symphony orchestra to supply the music. It was small wonder that Mrs. Oliver Hazard Perry Belmont complained, "I know of no profession, art, or trade that women are working in today, as taxing on mental resource as being a leader of Society."

*Mrs. George Gould bears up handsomely under the weight of a $500,000 pearl necklace. Her husband inherited a share of the $77 million estate of his father, Jay Gould.*

*A block-long town house, built by Cornelius Vanderbilt in Flamboyant Gothic, was one of the four Vanderbilt mansions that graced Fifth Avenue in New York.*

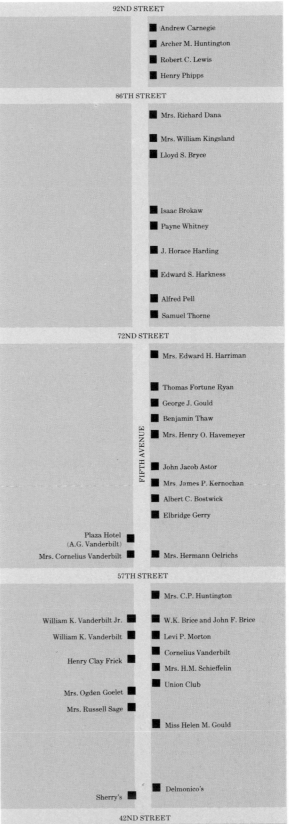

*Upper Fifth Avenue was New York's Gold Coast; the wealthy lined it with "French" châteaux and "Rhine" castles that excited the envy of anybody who wished to be somebody and the revulsion of those architects who advocated native originality. The map above locates some of the mansions and playgrounds of the Very Rich.*

*Two coaches pass on a tree-lined drive. Etiquette for such encounters was strict: on first meeting, one bowed; on second, one smiled; on third, one looked away.*

*A duchess by marriage but dressed like a queen, Consuelo Vanderbilt wears the coronet of her husband's house of Marlborough to the coronation of Edward VII.*

# The Bartered Brides

When Consuelo Vanderbilt announced that she was to wed the Duke of Marlborough, her brother Harold blurted out, "He is only marrying you for your money."

That, alas, barely needed saying. Consuelo's mother, like dozens of other American millionaires, wanted a nobleman for her daughter. There were many eager candidates among Europe's impoverished nobility.

Though Consuelo was unwilling, her mother forced her to go through with the nuptials. Her New York wedding was a spectacular affair. The church was adorned with thousands of yards of smilax and holly; it was crowded two hours before the choir sang "O! perfect love." Consuelo hung back for 20 minutes, alternately weeping and drying her tears, and when she finally appeared, "people were surprised to discover that she was fully half a head taller than the bridegroom."

Consuelo's marriage, like that of several other heiresses (overleaf), was far from a happy one. But there was this consolation: What American money had first joined together, it could almost as easily put asunder.

*A "Life" cartoon lampooned the figures in arranged matches: the heiress bound by her mother's will, the smallish nobleman, the preacher blind to the travesty.*

## The Duchess of Manchester
*Née Helena Zimmerman*

## The Duchess of Roxburghe
*Née May Goelet*

Eugene Zimmerman, a Cincinnati iron and oil millionaire, was surprised when he learned that his vacationing daughter Helena had eloped in November 1900 with a well-known English nobleman, the Duke of Manchester. Gamely said Mr. Zimmerman, "I have met the Duke, and was much impressed by his manly bearing." Others winked: Manchester, accused of "notorious dissipations and soiled reputation," had just been forced into bankruptcy. The marriage turned out to be a mixed bag. Surprisingly, it did last for 21 years, but the Zimmermans had to keep paying off the Duke's bills for lavish entertainment and world travel.

Lovely May Goelet, who had an Astor and a Vanderbilt in her family tree and also inherited millions in New York real estate, gallivanted through England rejecting the suits of sundry impoverished noblemen, none of whom seemed to interest her quite as much as one Captain Oswald Ames, a stalwart of the Horse Guards. In 1903, May settled wisely for the Duke of Roxburghe, who was gentlemanly, intelligent and well-to-do. After their marriage, the couple resided at Floors Castle, Roxburghe's 60,500-acre estate on the Scottish border. Their life was one of such domestic tranquillity that some of their aristocratic visitors tended to find them boring.

## The Princess de Sagan

*Née Anna Gould*

Though Anna Gould surely was not the prettiest of American heiresses, she had no trouble in acquiring two titled husbands. The first was Count Boni de Castellane, a dapper French spendthrift; he cost the Goulds some $5.5 million before the match was dissolved in 1906. Two years later, Anna fared better. She married Boni's rich and charming cousin Helie de Talleyrand-Périgord, Prince de Sagan, and later to be Duc de Talleyrand, whom she had met at Château de Marais, one of Boni's estates. Recalling Helie's visit, Boni wrote indignantly, "Little did I dream that he would eventually own Marais and—incidentally—marry my wife."

## The Countess of Yarmouth

*Née Alice Thaw*

Handsome Alice Thaw, of the Pittsburgh railroad-and-coke Thaws, met the impecunious Earl of Yarmouth at a party in Washington, D.C. According to the Pittsburgh *Post*, "he decided he couldn't exist happily without her," and when Alice left town to visit in Florida, "he boarded a train south so opportunely that the pair traveled on the same train." After a spectacular wedding, the couple headed for a honeymoon in England, hotly pursued by a marshal eager to attach the Earl's baggage in lieu of bad debts. Adding to the commotion was the scandalous absence of Alice's brother Harry, who soon perpetrated an even greater scandal *(overleaf)*.

*Evelyn Nesbit, the chorus-girl wife of Harry Thaw, testified in his defense. But beneath her innocent beauty one spectator said he detected "an ice-cold brain."*

# Scandal of the Decade

On June 25, 1906, socialite Harry K. Thaw shot to death the famous architect Stanford White for attempting to continue a flagrant dalliance with Thaw's bride, the winsome chorus girl Evelyn Nesbit *(left)*. The murder trial began in January 1907, and after weeks of lurid testimony, it ended with a hung jury. Thaw was retried the next year and adjudged "not guilty because insane." The high point of the whole affair came when Evelyn testified in her husband's defense. Her performance, intended to establish Thaw's forgivable instability, is indicated below in excerpts from the trial transcript. As the scene begins, Evelyn has just described how she declined Thaw's first proposal of marriage with the confession that White had "ruined" her when she was 16.

HARRY K. THAW

STANFORD WHITE

*Lawyer: What was the effect of this statement of yours upon Mr. Thaw?*

*Evelyn: He became very excited.*

*Lawyer: Will you kindly describe it?*

*Evelyn: He would get up and walk up and down the room a minute and then sit down and say, "Oh, God! Oh, God!" and bite his nails, and keep sobbing.*

*Lawyer: Sobbing?*

*Evelyn: Yes, it was not like crying. It was a deep sob. He kept saying, "Go on, go on, tell me the whole thing."*

*Lawyer: How long did that scene last, Mrs. Thaw?*

*Evelyn: Why, we stayed there all night. Every now and then he would come to me and ask me some particular thing about it.*

*Lawyer: In what direction were these questions?*

*Evelyn: He tried to find out whether Mama knew anything about it, and I said she did not. He thought, like a great many other people, that Mr. White was a very noble man. He told me that any decent person who heard that story would say it was not my fault. That I was simply a poor, unfortunate little girl, and that he did not think anything less of me. But on the contrary, he said that I must always remember he would be my friend, and no matter what happened, he would always be my friend.*

*Lawyer: When was it after that he renewed his proposal of marriage?*

*Evelyn: Later on. It was maybe two months after that he made up his mind and he was going to marry me anyway.*

*Lawyer: Will you please state to the jury that conversation?*

*Evelyn: I told him several times after that that even if I didn't marry him the friends of Stanford White would always laugh at him and make fun of him. I said marriage would not be a good thing—that I had been on the stage and I had been to a great many apartments with Stanford White.*

*Lawyer: What did he say to all these reasons of yours?*

*Evelyn: He kept saying he could not care for anybody else and could not possibly love anybody else; that his whole life was ruined; and he said he never would marry anyone else.*

*"The Breakers" cost Cornelius Vanderbilt $5 million before he bought a stick of furniture. Over its library fireplace was the motto, "Little do I care for riches."*

## The Place to Be

In 1908, a tip-sheet for millionaire social climbers rated the resorts of the Very Rich. At the top of the list was glittering Newport—and the advice "be very careful." For here the plutocracy spent at a rate that could exhaust even a fair-sized fortune in a single season of eight to ten weeks.

The requisites for a summer in Newport began with a house, which the Very Rich called, without humor, a cottage. A cottage of 30 rooms could be built or bought for under a million dollars, but the architectural whims of the wealthy often ran up much greater expenses. Coal baron E. J. Berwind managed to spend nearly $1.5 million on his cottage, "The Elms," but he was definitely put in the shade by the William K. Vanderbilts, who built their "Marble House" (*opposite*) for $2 million

and furnished it for $9 million. Even so, many connoisseurs held that the most luxurious of the cottages was Cornelius Vanderbilt's 70-room Renaissance palace, "The Breakers." A life-style befitting these mansions involved correspondingly fabulous sums. The biggest item was entertaining. Mrs. Pembroke Jones spent $300,000 a season on dinners and dances, and she was not the most imaginative of Newport hostesses. One candidate for that accolade was Mrs. Cornelius Vanderbilt; in 1902, it was her inspired fancy to import the whole cast of a New York hit, *The Wild Rose*, and to stage the show on her own lawn. But for sheer novelty, no one reached the heights—or the depths—of Harry Lehr, who invited 100 dogs and their masters to a banquet featuring fricassee of bones and shredded dog biscuit.

*"Marble House,"* an $11 million gift from William K. Vanderbilt to his wife, was built of marble imported from Africa, and had a ballroom paneled in gold.

A setting for gourmands, the dining room of W.K. Vanderbilt's Newport cottage, "Marble House," had solid bronze furniture and walls of Algerian marble.

# The High Cost of Being Rich

Newport society invented innumerable charming ways to keep its initiates terribly busy while absolutely idle. One might explore the countryside in small caravans of electric autos, to which the elegant ladies often gave endearing names, such as "Angelica" and "Puff-Puff." Alternatively, a game of croquet or a horseback canter was always in fashion.

The chief centers for open-air pursuits were Bailey's Beach and the Newport Casino. The Casino, where there were tennis matches and horse shows to attend, was awesomely difficult to join as a formal member. So, too, was Bailey's Beach. If a social-climbing stranger tried to crash his way onto the beach he was ejected by a discerning watchman, who would point out the way to plebeian Easton's Beach. But acceptable guests were regaled with sights to write home about. There was Mr. James Van Alen, entering the surf wearing a monocle and puffing a fine cigar. And here was Mrs. Oliver Hazard Perry Belmont, breasting the breakers while protecting her complexion with a charming green parasol. It was all great fun. And, of course, it was all expensive. But if one was clever, he might be able to get by on the modest budget suggested below in excerpts from a 1907 article in *The Cosmopolitan* magazine.

*Newport is the most expensive city in the world; it's twice as expensive as New York," declares a friend who spends eight thousand dollars a season for the rent of his cottage. A fashionable family will easily spend a thousand dollars a month in the season simply on flowers for small dinners.*

*I asked what it costs one of these ladies whose duty it is to shine in Newport for her gowns.*

*"Ten thousand dollars a year," he answered promptly. "If a woman spends only five thousand a year, we do not take her very seriously." And I was left to imagine what might be the ladies' bills for hats, boots, lingerie, etc.*

*What is a smart automobile stable and what does it cost? John Jacob Astor has had as many as 17 at one time. I am told that four automobiles are a satisfactory number. Two chauffeurs and a helper are required, and the running expenses reach seven hundred dollars a month.*

*A general impression of the cost and complexity of a quiet Newport establishment may be obtained by glancing over the following specimen payroll (I am not speaking now of the richest families, whose payrolls would of course be much larger):*

| OCCUPATION | YEARLY SALARY |
|---|---|
| Special chef from Paris | $5,000 |
| Second chef | 1,200 |
| Private secretary to the lady | 3,000 |
| Private tutor | 2,000 |
| Governess | 1,000 |
| Two nurses | 1,000 |
| Housekeeper | 1,000 |
| Five maids | 1,200 |
| Head coachman | 1,200 |
| Second and third coachmen | 1,200 |
| Chauffeur | 1,000 |
| Butler | 900 |
| Second butler | 600 |
| Head gardener | 1,000 |
| Four helpers | 2,500 |
| Total | $23,800 |

*Promenading on the Newport greensward, Miss Louise Scott (left) and Mrs. Gordon Douglass enjoy a key activity of the resort: observing and being observed.*

COMMODORE C. VANDERBILT

## *Regal Seafarers*

In Newport, yachting rather than horse racing was the sport of kings; indeed, nothing less than a king's ransom would buy a vessel of acceptable size and comfort. Cornelius Vanderbilt *(above)* paid about $250,000 for the *North Star (right)*, and every year the expenses of simply making the boat run put him at least another $20,000 or so out of pocket. The yacht owners expected speed as well as luxury for their money; if a boat could not keep up with its rivals, it was simply scrapped for a new one. Albert C. Burrage built one of the most impressive with money from Chilean copper mines. His *Aztec* could make 18.5 knots, and it carried 270 tons of coal, enough to travel 5,500 miles without a stop.

No less impressive than their performance and cost were the steam yachts' interiors. High ceilings, skylights, paneled walls and parquet floors combined to give the impression that the owner had simply launched his mansion for a leisurely cruise. Many yacht owners had fully appointed offices on board, complete with a wireless to keep them in touch with Wall Street.

To yachtsmen, this prodigal effort and expense were eminently worthwhile, for nothing could compare with the pleasure of a brisk cruise in luxurious privacy. Financier J. P. Morgan, who ran through three big yachts aptly named *Corsair*, broke his customary silence to elaborate on the mystique of sailing. "You can do business with anybody," he said gruffly, "but you can only sail a boat with a gentleman." In keeping with this stern dictum, Morgan usually cast off with fewer than four men—not counting, of course, his 85-man crew.

*The dining room of "North Star" was richly done with Louis XIV furniture.*

*The 256-foot yacht "North Star" ferried the Vanderbilts between Newport and New York City, or took the family across the Atlantic to their European residences.*

*Mrs. Vanderbilt's stateroom was one of nine for guests and family members.*

*In the library, Vanderbilt could relax beside a handsome but fake fireplace.*

The Very Rich enjoy a tennis match at the Newport Casino, where initial membership cost a mere $500, but keeping up appearances afterward might cost a fortune.

# The Motorcar

An early motorist tries to find his way home from the middle of nowhere.

# The Automobiling Fad

*A man who would now win the parvenu's bow must belong to the automobility.*

*LIFE*, 1901

In 1900, America had only 8,000 cars. Yet almost everyone was fascinated by the frail, costly, balky contraptions that, as one owner described them, "shook and trembled and clattered, spat oil, fire, smoke, and smell." People with fat wallets and a taste for adventure—especially nice, safe adventure—began buying these new machines, running all over the place in them and setting new standards of glamorous consumership. A whole automotive culture was being born, and with it, a brand-new vocabulary.

At the time it was not yet certain that the word "automobile" would triumph as a replacement for that awkward old phrase, "horseless carriage." A prize of $500 had recently been offered for a new generic name, and many people preferred the winner—"motocycle." Less favored coinages included "petrocar" and "viamote" and "mocle." The suggestion of "mobe"—pronounced "mobee"—prompted one newspaper to parody Shakespeare: "To mobe or not to mobe, that is the question." Another periodical suggested brightly, "Why not call it a 'goalone' and then let-it-alone?"

And what did one call the pilot and passenger of said vehicle? In the test of common usage, "automobilist" lost out to "motorist," and "chauffeur" (French for "stoker") gave way to "driver." Women, who took the wheel in increasing numbers, were tentatively called "chauffeuses." Almost at once, men decided that female drivers by any name were distinctly the deadlier of the species. This ungallant view inspired countless snappy jokes. For example:

"Papa, why is Mamma like a woman driver?"

"Because she's always running somebody down."

To control the driver of either sex, local traffic laws bloomed in baffling profusion. In 1902, the state of Vermont, apparently imitating an old English ordinance restricting steam carriages, required every auto to be preceded by a mature individual waving a red flag. In Tennessee, motorists had to post a week's notice before they could legally start out on a trip. But even the soundest of the new laws were broken, sometimes in ignorance, sometimes in flagrant disregard, and automotive bad manners came to be as commonplace as flat tires. Offenders were lectured sternly in a book called *Everyday Etiquette*, published in 1905. The book cautioned the well-bred motorist: "Do not stare at another's car, nor, if at a standstill, examine the mech-

AN EVIL AND THE REMEDY.

*The reckless motorist strews havoc in his wake. Though this driver is halted by the Law (inset), real-life offenders often managed to evade bicycle-mounted police.*

In deep trouble, a mudbound driver struggles to extricate his car. The standard solution for this problem was provided, embarrassingly, by a farmer's horse.

anism. This is the height of rudeness." A second warning was: "When passing an auto of inferior horsepower, do not choose that moment to exhibit your own greater speed." And another to the would-be marathon driver: "Do not boast of the phenomenal runs you have made. You are not a record-holder. And when you become one, the newspapers will gladly exploit the fact without any viva voce testimony from you."

Well-meant if ineffectual edicts from the guardians of public manners and safety were the least of the obstacles faced by the pioneer motorist. When he dared to venture beyond the city limits, he had to cope with the roads, only a small number of which were paved. He soon found himself in an uncharted wilderness of dirt roads and meandering country lanes. In these alien byways lurked perils great and small. If thick mud did not bespatter and ensnare the driver, clouds of dust choked and blinded him, concealing deep ruts and potholes that could easily throw a car out of control. If accident or breakdown occurred—and both frequently did —the motorist was left to act as his own mechanic in a world that had yet to see its first rural gas station.

The doughty drivers of the decade pooh-poohed the fears of doctors that these hazards would cause "acute mental suffering, nervous excitement, and circulatory disturbances." As for the physical demands of motoring, both male motorists and their allegedly delicate female companions showed themselves willing and able to wrestle with the worst of the dangers that either the road or the vehicle had to offer.

As things turned out, adversity only stimulated the craze for the automobile and everything that was connected with it. Americans turned out in great numbers to applaud a ludicrous melodrama, "The Great Automobile Mystery." They made popular songs of "The Automobile Honeymoon," "Toot Your Horn, Kid, You're in a Fog," and, of course, "In My Merry Oldsmobile" (page 259). Above all, they bought more and better cars— some 460,000 of them during the decade—and then drove off to enjoy a new and exciting life on wheels.

## A Fad Becomes Fancy

While automobiling began as a haphazard adventure, the equipage for the new fad quickly became as elaborate as that for an English duke's safari into Africa. By 1904 a New York store, Saks & Co., found motoring garb a subject so complex that it required a 270-page catalogue. The two Saks fashions shown here make it quite clear that women, as always, got the best of the couturier's art. The men, condemned to dusters resembling a chem-

### BASIC TOOLS AND SUPPLIES

**TOOLS**

2 Pair tire chains
1 Efficient jack
1 Brace wrench for
   changing rims
1 Efficient tire pump
1 Tire gauge
1 Valve tool
1 Small vulcanizer
1 Sheet fine sandpaper
1 Sheet fine emery cloth
All special wrenches
   belonging to car
2 Monkey wrenches
1 Small set socket wrenches
1 Small Stillson wrench
2 Screw drivers (one with all
   wooden handle)
1 Pair pliers with wire
   cutters
1 Good jackknife
1 Small vise to clamp to
   running board
1 12-oz. machinist's hammer

1 Punch or carpenter's
   nail set
1 Cotter-pin extractor
1 Large flat mill file
1 Thin knife-edged file
1 Small short-handled axe
1 Towing cable
1 Oil squirt can
1 Grease gun
1 Small funnel
1 Chamois skin
1 Small ball of marline
1 Pocket electric flashlight
   (if car has no trouble lam
1 Pocket ammeter

**SPARE PARTS & EXTRA**

1 or 2 Extra tire casings an
   inner tubes
1 Strong two-gallon can
   extra gasoline
1 Strong two-quart sealabl
   can gas-engine oil
1 Can grease
1 Small sealable can kerose

ist's laboratory coat, sought consolation in a catalogue that was no less encyclopedic, put out by New York's posh hardware store, Hammacher Schlemmer. In 1906 that catalogue urged every motorist to equip his car with a basic outfit of 35 tools, which could be bought for a mere $25.00. After a few more years of automotive inflation, a magazine recommended for the minimal motoring kit the formidable array of items listed below.

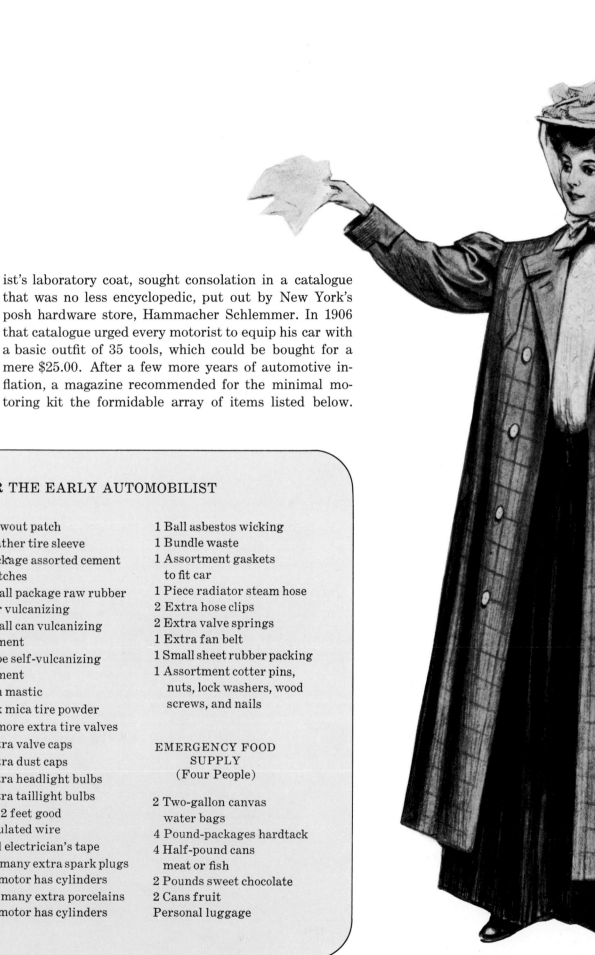

## FOR THE EARLY AUTOMOBILIST

Blowout patch
Leather tire sleeve
Package assorted cement
 patches
Small package raw rubber
 for vulcanizing
Small can vulcanizing
 cement
Tube self-vulcanizing
 cement
Can mastic
Box mica tire powder
 or more extra tire valves
Extra valve caps
Extra dust caps
Extra headlight bulbs
Extra taillight bulbs
to 12 feet good
 insulated wire
Roll electrician's tape
⁄₂ as many extra spark plugs
 as motor has cylinders
⁄₂ as many extra porcelains
 as motor has cylinders

1 Ball asbestos wicking
1 Bundle waste
1 Assortment gaskets
 to fit car
1 Piece radiator steam hose
2 Extra hose clips
2 Extra valve springs
1 Extra fan belt
1 Small sheet rubber packing
1 Assortment cotter pins,
 nuts, lock washers, wood
 screws, and nails

EMERGENCY FOOD
SUPPLY
(Four People)

2 Two-gallon canvas
 water bags
4 Pound-packages hardtack
4 Half-pound cans
 meat or fish
2 Pounds sweet chocolate
2 Cans fruit
Personal luggage

*A prosperous country family proudly poses in its brand-new Haynes Touring Car, which cost about $3,000 to buy and probably another $3,000 each year to run.*

*The 1908 Packard exemplified the early trend toward big and elegant cars with polished brass trim.*

## Rich Man's Toy

*Nothing has spread socialistic feeling in this country more than the use of the automobile. To the countryman, they are a picture of the arrogance of wealth, with all its independence and carelessness.* WOODROW WILSON

By 1906, when the anxious statement above was issued by the president of Princeton, the recklessness of wealthy motorists had indeed aroused widespread resentment. Rich folk on their way to spas and shore resorts casually ran down livestock and drove on as fast as possible. In the cities, pedestrians were angered by the dangerous driving of millionaires like Alfred Gwynne Vanderbilt, who raced his red touring car through New York at reckless speeds of more than 10 miles an hour. Moreover, the plutocrats used their cars to flaunt their wealth. As a magazine article reported, one rich member of an auto club "had the lamps on his Panhard gold plated, and on each of them the club emblem blazed. The emblems were solid gold, set with rubies."

Nevertheless, those who feared a socialistic backlash missed the mark by 180 degrees. The object of resentment became a symbol of success, coveted even by poor pedestrians; the automobile was admired all the more as new models incorporated greater elegance. Oldsmobile and other manufacturers prospered by making frank appeals to the pride of newly affluent people. The opulent car was usually powerful, and a few automakers began bragging about the speed of their products, as proved by glamorous races. But the car of the decade was the last word in elegance—the Great Arrow *(page 238);* it was so prestigious that its advertising snobbishly omitted all mention of cost ($4,500 up). Whoever had to ask the cost obviously could not afford a Great Arrow.

*A glorious vision of speed, a 1910 Oldsmobile outraces a railroad train in an ad demonstrating the illusion of surging power that a mere $3,000 could purchase.*

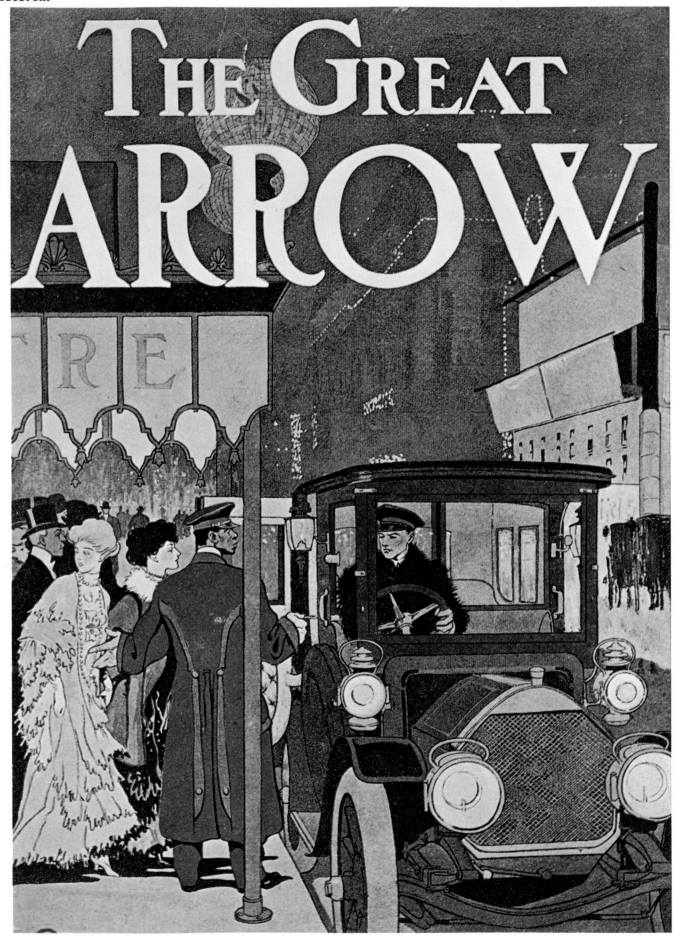

THE GREAT ARROW

*The Great Arrow was so sure of its stature that some ads, like this one in 1907, grandly omitted not only the price but any description of the car.*

*By 1910 the Arrow had a more modest name—but just as much snob appeal.*

*Competing for the quality buyer, Peerless traded on its grandiloquent name.*

*The Baker pioneered in aiming its sales pitch of safety to women drivers.*

*Columbia ads stressed traveling, as in this illustration of a European tour.*

# The Triumph of the Locomobile

The finish of the 1908 International Race for the Vanderbilt Cup. Won by the 90 H.P. Locomobile at an average speed of 64.38 miles an hour, breaking all records established in competition for this celebrated trophy. A victory for the Locomobile a triumph for the entire American automobile industry. The striking poster illustrated above is lithographed in eleven colors. Suitable for framing, with or without descriptive matter. Mailed on receipt of 10 cents.

## 1909 *Locomobile Cars*

The "30" LOCOMOBILE – A new five passenger model with a shaft drive system, thoroughly developed through three years of road testing. The name, Locomobile, on a shaft drive car guarantees its superiority.  $3500

The "40" LOCOMOBILE – A seven passenger car, safe and comfortable – ideal for family use. The logical choice of those who want a high powered car.  $4500

INFORMATION ON APPLICATION

The *Locomobile* Company of America. Bridgeport Conn.
BRANCHES
NEW YORK – BOSTON – CHICAGO – PHILADELPHIA

*An ad for the Locomobile, winner of the 1908 Vanderbilt Cup race, shifted the emphasis from elegance to speed as pioneer auto races caught the public fancy.*

*Drivers rev up their motors for the start of the 1909 Indianapolis race. The 100-mile event was won by Louis Strang, with an average speed of 64 miles per hour.*

*Florodora Sextette and swains sing "Tell Me, Pretty Maiden," in "Florodora," the hit of 1900.*

# *A Thousand Hits, Count 'Em*

*Introducing in a 15-minute act, juggling, unicycling, magic, hand balancing, rag-time piano and violin playing, dancing, globe rolling, wirewalking, talking and cartooning. Something original in each line—SOME ENTERTAINMENT!*

ADVERTISEMENT FOR A ONE-MAN VAUDEVILLE ACT

America was ravenous for entertainment as the new century got under way, and show business responded with a richer, more varied fare than the country had ever seen. Movies, sometimes called "flickering flicks" were in a groping infancy (a 1902 newsreel faked the eruption of a volcano by showing a beer barrel exploding in the sun). Spectacular circuses traveled from city to city in special trains of as many as 90 railway cars at a time. An inspired Tin Pan Alley sold two billion copies of sheet music in the single year 1910.

The legitimate stage achieved an all-time high of activity with more than 400 stock and touring companies carrying drama to the nation, and four or five plays opening on Broadway on an ordinary night. Many of these plays were of a new, earthy texture, and theater audiences, long used to lofty Shakespearean repertory and melodramas of the Jack Dalton genre, sometimes found themselves being brought down too far too fast. When, in a daring new production called *The City*, the word "goddam" was abruptly uttered—for the first time on a Broadway stage—the audience rose for an intermission in such horror and hysteria that the New York *Sun* critic fainted dead away in the ensuing crush.

For the average man of the decade, the favorite entertainment was vaudeville. Practically every town in the country had a vaudeville theater. Sometimes the performances lived up to their billing, and sometimes they did not even come close. Solid comedy acts like The Three Keatons *(right)*, with young Buster as The Human Mop, delighted audiences with their patter and knockabout acrobatics. On the other hand, reaction was decidedly mixed to the usual vaudeville collection of ventriloquists, jugglers, singers and animal acts. The standard gags from rapid-fire comics—"I sent my wife to the Thousand Islands for a vacation: a week on each island" or "You can drive a horse to drink, but a pencil must be lead"—might receive any response from belly laughs to stony silence. And the Cherry Sisters, billed with awful irony as "America's Worst Act" (though the sisters insisted they were great), were indeed so bad that they always sang behind a net, which protected them from elderly fruit and vegetables thrown by the audience. On the following pages is a sample of these performers, some of them the finest in the history of American theater. Others, like Adgie and Her Lions and the Southern Four, enjoyed merited obscurity.

*In 1901, six-year-old Buster Keaton did a vaudeville skit in which he teased his parents—who were, in fact, his real mother and father.*

MARIE DRESSLER

HARRY LAUDER

THE SOUTHERN FOUR

LEW FIELDS

LOIE FULLER

EVA TANGUAY

W. C. FIELDS

JOE WEBER

ADGIE AND HER LION

*Bandits escape with the mail in one of the 14 scenes of "The Great Train Robbery," whose famed director, Edwin S. Porter, pioneered in film editing.*

## A New Entry in Show Biz

In 1903 a 12-minute epic called *The Great Train Robbery* became the first truly suspenseful movie. Photographed at a Lackawanna freight yard in Paterson, New Jersey, it set a permanent style for dramas that were depicted in several scenes. Within five years, 10,000 stores across the nation were converted into nickelodeons, small theaters that offered movies for a five-cent admission price.

*Notices to the audience periodically appeared on the nickelodeon screens.*

# Constellation
## of
## Leading Ladies

*Some shone with a crackling brilliance and others with a mysterious glow, but together these stars filled the American legitimate stage with an array of talent rarely excelled in any age.*

**Maxine Elliott**

*She conquered audiences with her beauty, which sometimes*
*overshadowed her acting skill. The painter Whistler proclaimed*
*her "the Girl with the Midnight Eyes," and Ethel Barrymore*
*said she was "the Venus de Milo—with arms."*

### Minnie Maddern Fiske

Great actors, she once said, "have, in a sense, always played
themselves." Revealingly, she chose to act in serious, intelligent
plays, and she popularized Ibsen. Her genius was to convey
emotion with a minimum of voice and gesture.

**Julia Marlowe**

*Spurning modern drama, she played Shakespearean heroines
with the authority of a scholar—which, in fact, she was. Of
her performance in "Romeo and Juliet," an awed critic wrote
that she "was not only lovely as Juliet, she was Juliet."*

**Ethel Barrymore**

*Strong yet sensitive, she was the steady center of a tempestuous theater family. When she scored her first hit in 1901 ("the newest princess of our footlit realm," said a critic), countless girls began to try to imitate her warm, throaty voice.*

### *Maude Adams*

*The most popular actress of the day, she captured the
hearts of playgoers with a wistful, fragile manner. When, as Peter
Pan, she asked in a small voice, "Do you believe in fairies?"
the enchanted audience never failed to cry, "Yes!"*

# A Word from the Critics

The annual display of limbs, lungs and lingerie which Florenz Ziegfeld brings to town under the title of "The Parisian Model," with his wife Anna Held as the star feature of the exhibition, packed the Illinois Theater to the roof last night. It is billed to remain for four weeks and the management looks forward to a solid month of financial joy, furnished by the class of theater-goers who happen to like that sort of thing and feel assured that Miss Held's organization of "show girls" under the astute management of young Mr. Ziegfeld, will give them just what they like. An enterprising laundry solicitor might do a good stroke of business by getting around to the Illinois Theater early today. Some of the lingerie that was so generously and abundantly displayed by the energetic young women is sadly in need of the tub.

CHICAGO *EXAMINER*, FEBRUARY 10, 1909

With the force of the hurricanes and mighty storms on the hills comes a slum romance by Edward Sheldon, "Salvation Nell," and a crowded house sat breathless or in profound sympathy either with the scarlet sort of bitter humor, the tender moments or big palpitating tragedies which rage in brief fierceness like chain lightning. Mrs. Fiske, in the manner of a slender ribbon of pale, sweet light, brings to the part of Nell, the saved girl of the slums, a little strange face with a look of dawn upon it and a voice of spring. The drama is a big splashing crash of brute entanglements, a study in anger and poverty, in vice, ignorance, and the terrible truths of snarled, vagrant, untutored, godless life. Its gravities are accusatory and threatening, its realism is vivid, its humor broad and thoroughly American and its pathos deep as the snows upon the Alpine passes. It is the most interesting melodrama in all time.

CHICAGO *DAILY NEWS*, FEBRUARY 16, 1909

The dramatization of "Rebecca of Sunnybrook Farm" is almost fairylike in its daintiness and imaginative charm. Once in a great while, only, does one encounter such delightful simplicity in events, dialogue and character interpretation as are found in this play. There is sunshine and sweetness in this play that is never overdrawn.

*VOGUE*, NOVEMBER 15, 1910

Booth Tarkington has done the miracle. He has put new wine in old bottles without bursting the bottles or spoiling the wine. His play "A Man From Home" is served, to be sure, in a framework of melodrama which has done duty for a century, but the threadbare plot serves well enough as a foundation for Mr. Tarkington's message of the superiority of honest homespun American ways and of the home folks to the sort of Europeans whom young Americans going abroad with too much money are likely to find themselves surrounded by.

BROOKLYN *EAGLE*, NOVEMBER 16, 1909

The Journal calls the attention of the police to the play "Sapho" given here last night at Wallack's Theater by Miss Olga Nethersole. It is with regret that the Journal does this, but there is a public duty to be performed here—it is the duty of the authorities to call a halt. A great many improper plays have been given in New York recently. "Sapho" is the limit —it should not be performed again. If the police do not interfere no man or woman who values his or her good name should ever go to a performance. A large audience, apparently incapable of understanding what they said, applauded vehemently as Miss Nethersole grovelled in the dust at the feet of her youthful, but caddish lover! "Sapho" is, after all, a cold-blooded bid for the sensual approval of foolish people.

NEW YORK *JOURNAL*, FEBRUARY 6, 1900

*Anna Held, the coquettish French star of musical comedy, was once accused by a blue-nosed critic of causing sexual unrest with her lovely legs and 18-inch waist.*

## *Medley for an Epoch*

In the easy-going, almost unembarrassable mood of the first decade, song writers tapped practically every emotion—and subject—in their efforts to score a hit. Pride in the technology of the age was evoked by songs like "In My Merry Oldsmobile" and "Come, Josephine, in My Flying Machine." Hearts were wrung by ballads such as "A Bird in a Gilded Cage" (the composer tested it out in a brothel to see if it would make the girls cry). Patriotic sentiment surged at the sound of George M. Cohan's "You're a Grand Old Flag," originally titled "You're a Grand Old Rag." Filial virtue found

expression in "Next to Your Mother, Who Do You Love?"

The fountainhead of inspiration for the composers of the day was Tin Pan Alley, a block of 28th Street in New York City named for the sound of pianos pounding all day long. Music publishers on the Alley ground out thousands of tunes each year, but the business of picking a winner was woefully imprecise. Tin Pan Alley almost turned down "In the Good Old Summer Time" because publishers thought it would have audience appeal for only three months of the year. To their amazement, it sold a million copies in the first 12 months.

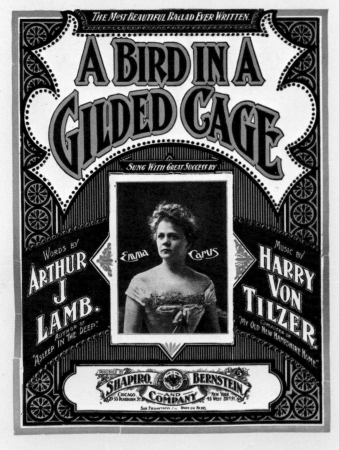

1900

1910

1901

1902

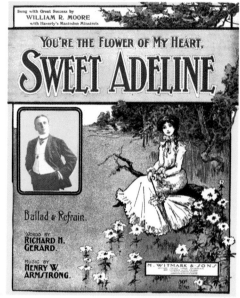

1903

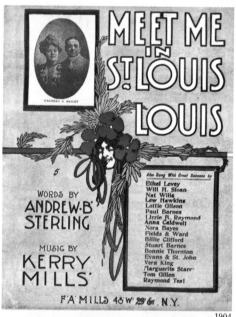

1904

1905

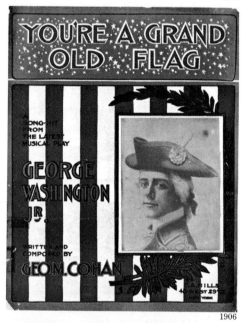

1906

1907

1908

1909

Fierce animals, trained to perfect obedience, were a lure of Barnum & Bailey posters pasted up around towns and cities on the circus tour.

Ringling Brothers' posters boasted of equine acts for, as Alf Ringling once said, "A circus without horses would be like a kite without a tail."

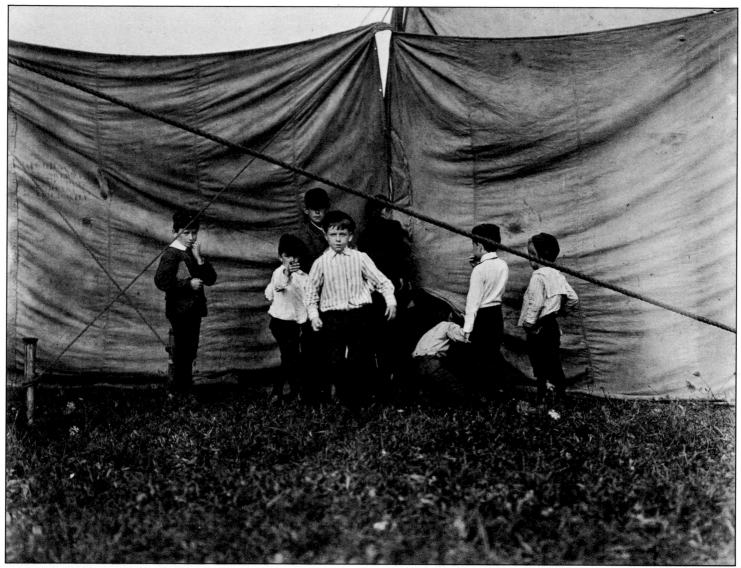

*Young boys, surprised here by a photographer as they make an attempt to sneak under a canvas barrier, were surely the most avid and resourceful of circus fans.*

# The Big Top

Nothing in show business could match the excitement of a circus parade as it rolled through town luring customers with a display of ornately carved wagons, lumbering elephants *(overleaf)* and a calliope or "steam organ"—which brought up the rear because its boiler sometimes blew up. Dozens of circuses toured America, but the two giants were the Ringling Brothers Circus and Barnum & Bailey's, each striving to be recognized as the greatest show in the world. Barnum & Bailey's claimed to have an unexcelled "congress of wild beasts" in its menagerie. Ringling Brothers once asserted that it had the only giraffe left in the world.

The competition raised entertainment to dizzying peaks. The circuses put on spectacular plays, such as the Ringling Brothers' "Jerusalem and the Crusades," which used lavish scenery, hundreds of animals and more than a thousand performers. The three rings under the big top swarmed with clowns, lion trainers and high-wire gymnasts. Ernest Clarke, the fabulous trapeze artist, thrilled onlookers with his triple somersault. Isabella Butler rode in a toy automobile that sped down a ramp, turned upside down and shot "into space forty feet away across a veritable chasm of death." In the words of Barnum & Bailey's program, the audience reaction to such sights was bound to be pure awe: "Your heart still palpitates. 'This is the limit,' you say."

*A herd of elephants, considered by P. T. Barnum to be the very heart of a circus, brings up the rear of a mile-long parade through Manchester, New Hampshire.*

# Summer Days

*Vacationing girls wade beneath San Francisco's brooding Cliff House restaurant.*

## The Good Old Summertime

*Summer afternoon—summer afternoon; to me those have always been the two most beautiful words in the English language.*

HENRY JAMES, AS QUOTED BY EDITH WHARTON

"There's nothing like the good old summer time," mused the song writer and vaudeville star George "Honey Boy" Evans in 1902, during an alfresco luncheon with fellow musicians at Brighton Beach, near New York. Apparently the rest of the nation agreed; Evans' casual remark, given a lilting melody and a set of lyrics, became one of the most popular songs of the decade.

There was no doubt, in fact, that summer was the season people loved best. For children it conjured up images of Fourth of July parades, baseball games, a favorite swimming hole or a romp in a haystack *(opposite)*. For their parents, it meant carefree outings in the countryside, excursions to trolley parks, perhaps a trip to one of the decade's "World's Fairs," and, most important of all, a chance to take part in a brand new American institution—the two-week summer vacation.

With the first warm weather, thousands of Americans began a migration to resort hotels in the mountains or at the seashore. Though accommodations were often cramped, the vacationers' mood was as expansive and carefree as the ocean itself. "Everything goes in summer," was the popular phrase, despite the cautionary advice of a popular etiquette book that "promiscuous

intimacies at summer resorts are a great mistake!"

Many summer watering spots were decidedly honky-tonk. "Atlantic City," said *Cosmopolitan*, "is the eighth wonder of the world. It is overwhelming in its crudeness." Lining its sandy beach was "a lunatic's dream of peep-shows, cigar shops, merry-go-rounds, hotels, bazaars, fortune tellers' booths [and] seven miles of board walk crowded with forty thousand human beings."

For those who could not travel, the same sort of carnival excitement could be found at trolley parks near the edges of almost every large city. Built by street car companies to attract fares, these gaudy establishments, with their Ferris wheels, band concerts, baseball games, vaudeville acts and boating ponds, offered both recreation and relief from the oppressive heat of the city. Half the fun, it seemed, was getting there—the pleasure of the cooling breeze produced by the speeding trolley car on its way to the park.

But despite its thrills and excitements, the real enjoyments of summer were the simple ones—the chance to get out of doors, to stroll down a tree-shaded lane and to experience the general feeling that times were good and life in America was indeed worth living.

*Caught in the carefree mood of the summer season, a group of playful youngsters grin impishly from the middle of a haystack in a field in Pawling, New York.*

*The most spectacular fair of the decade, the St. Louis World's Fair of 1904, attracted nearly 20 million visitors and inspired a song hit: "Meet Me in St. Louis."*

In the first decade, America proudly put on five so-called "World's Fairs" or major regional expositions. Vacationers flocked to these gaudy shows, to wander down the midway or marvel at the flamboyant buildings with their wondrous exhibits—Japanese gardens, American airships and strange new electrical gadgets such as automatic dishwashers.

*At the Seattle Exposition of 1909, one weight-guessing game lures a lone customer and his solemn companion.*

*Sunday picnickers take advantage of the warm weather to feast off hampers full of cold chicken, sandwiches and soda pop at the edge of a Minnesota cornfield.*

*Sporting the latest, most revealing in scratchy wool and linen beach-wear styles, a platoon of bathers frolic at the water's edge at Atlantic City, New Jersey.*

*For a little boy, summer was a magic time of safe adventure, exploring with a small friend the weed-strewn wonders of the oceanside, or daring to clamber in the branches of a tall tree with a larger friend who would never, never let you fall.*

*A pair of young straw-hatted friends, hand-in-hand, watch the receding tide of the Pacific.*

*Handsomely dressed in his Sunday best, a small Midwestern adventurer gently eases himself into the fork of a tree—and thence onto the lap of his indulgent uncle.*

*Thirsty electric workers belly up to the punch table for some freshly squeezed orangeade and lemonade during their Third Annual Outing on August 26, 1906.*

Midsummer weather softened the corporate heart of many an otherwise gruff employer, who sometimes made it a practice to treat his staff to an outing in the countryside. Employees and their families, like these wards of the Milwaukee Electric Railway and Light Company, who rode specially hired trolley cars to Waukesha Beach, Wisconsin, had a full day of picnicking, ball games, potato races—and gallon after gallon of soft drinks and beer.

*In a festive mood for their outing, employees disembark from a train of flag-decked trolley cars.*

*Summer Days*

*An Independence Day float, draped in bunting and carrying much of the population of Big Fork, Minnesota, was a main feature of the July Fourth celebration.*

A sudden gust on White Bear Lake, Minnesota, meant a dunking for all—including one seemingly disembodied arm and a girl who brought along her umbrella.

# Credits

*The sources for the illustrations which appear in this book are shown below. Credits for the pictures from left to right are separated by semicolons, from top to bottom by dashes.*

7—J. A. Schuck, University of Oklahoma Library (A. Y. Owen)—Culver Pictures. 8—Brown Brothers—Nebraska State Historical Society; Culver Pictures. 9—Cincinnati Historical Society; Bradley Smith—U.S. Navy Photo. 10,11—Chicago Historical Society. 12,13—Ford Archives: Henry Ford Museum, Dearborn, Michigan (Joe Clark). 14,15—State Historical Society of Wisconsin. 16,17—Cleveland Public Library. 18,19—Culver Pictures. 20,21—Minnesota Historical Society. 22,23—Fred O. Seibel. 24,25—Atlanta Historical Society. 26,27—Culver Pictures. 28—*The Daily News*, Chicago, December 31, 1900. 32,33—Courtesy the New-York Historical Society (Robert Crandall). 35—*The Boston Post*, January 1, 1901. 36,37—Manchester Historical Society. 39,40,41—Marie Cosindas. 42,43—Pennell Collection, University of Kansas. 44,45—Collection of Fred and Jo Mazzulla. 46,47—Courtesy Mrs. Lillia Saunders; The Baron de Hirsch Fund—Minnesota Historical Society. 48,49—Western Collection, Denver Public Library. 50,51—The Byron Collection, Museum of the City of New York. 53,54—Brown Brothers. 55—Courtesy the Hearst Corporation. 56—Bostwick-Frohardt Collection, owned by KMTV, Omaha. 57—Culver Pictures. 58—Edward Steichen, Museum of Modern Art. 59—Bettmann Archive. 60—Edward Steichen, Museum of Modern Art. 63—Bettmann Archive. 64—Library of Congress—Theodore Roosevelt Birthplace. 65—Frances B. Johnston, Library of Congress—Culver Pictures. 66,67—Frances B. Johnston, Library of Congress. 68—Theodore Roosevelt Birthplace—Edward S. Curtis, Library of Congress. 69—Edward S. Curtis, Library of Congress—American Museum of Natural History. 70,71—Culver Pictures. 73—Brown Brothers. 74,75—New York Public Library. 76,77—Library of Congress except top middle Culver Pictures. 78,79—Lewis W. Hine, George Eastman House. 80,81—Chicago Historical Society. 82—*The Literary Digest*, November 25, 1905. 83—Cleveland Public Library. 84,85—Lewis W. Hine, George Eastman House. 86,87—Underwood & Underwood. 89—National Air and Space Museum, Smithsonian Institution. 90,91—Culver Pictures (2); Brown Brothers; Culver Pictures (2); Brown Brothers. 92,93—Kansas State Historical Society. 94—From *A History of Flight* by Courtlandt Canby, Charles Dollfus Collection. 95—From *A Pictorial History of Aviation* by the editors of *Year*, (Photo World)—letter from *St. Nicholas* © 1908, The Century Co., reprinted by permission of Appleton-Century-Crofts, Division of Meredith Corp. 96,97—United Press International. 98,99—Clarke Historical Library, Central Michigan University. 101—Culver Pictures and Sy Seidman (Robert Crandall photo composition). 102 through 105—© King Features Syndicate 1907, 1909, Sy Seidman. 106,107—Sy Seidman and Culver Pictures (Robert Crandall photo composition). 108—Sy Seidman. 110—Marie Cosindas. 112,113—Drawings from: *The American Girls Handy Book* and *The American Boys Handy Book*. 114,115—Minnesota Historical Society. 116,117—Frances B. Johnston, Culver Pictures. 118,119—City News Bureau Photo, St. Petersburg, Florida. 120,121—L. C. McClure, Western Collection, Denver Public Library. 122 through 135—Kansas State Historical Society. 136 through 145—Pennell Collection, University of Kansas. 146—Chippewa Valley Historical Museum. 147—Marie Daerr, Cleveland, Ohio; Fisher Collection, State Historical Society of Wisconsin—Henry E. Huntington Library and Art Gallery; State Historical Society of Wisconsin. 148—Michigan Historical Commission, State Archives (2)—Henry E. Huntington Library and Art Gallery; Courtesy Mrs. Robert Crowe (J. R. Eyerman). 149—Courtesy Mrs. M. J. Kitterman; Michigan Historical Commission, State Archives—Chippewa Valley Historical Museum. 150—State Historical Society of Wisconsin—Henry E. Huntington Library and Art Gallery—State Historical Society of Wisconsin. 151—Rollins College Archives; State Historical Society of Wisconsin—Michigan Historical Commission, State Archives—State Historical Society of Wisconsin. 152—Courtesy Holland McCombs; Chippewa Valley Historical Museum—Henry E. Huntington Library and Art Gallery; Chippewa Valley Historical Museum.

153—Courtesy Mrs. Robert Crowe (J. R. Eyerman); Courtesy Holland McCombs—Minnesota Historical Society. 154,155—Culver Pictures. 157—Missouri Historical Society. 158,159—From *Ladies' Home Journal*, September 15, 1910, © The Curtis Publishing Co., Culver Pictures. 160,161—From *L'Art de la Mode*, February 1906, Sy Seidman. 162—From *Ladies' Home Journal*, July 1910, © The Curtis Publishing Co., Culver Pictures. 164—Culver Pictures. 165—Culver Pictures except bottom left Brown Brothers. 166,167—Text from *Ladies' Home Journal*, March 1908 © The Curtis Publishing Co. 168—Culver Pictures. 169—Items from the Bostwick-Braun Co. Hardware Catalogue, The Sears, Roebuck & Co. Catalogue, 1906-1907 and the Warshaw Collection. 170,171—South Dakota State Historical Society—Items from the Sears, Roebuck & Co. Catalogue 1906-1907. 172,173—Charles J. Van Schaick Collection, State Historical Society of Wisconsin—Items from the Sears, Roebuck & Co. Catalogue 1906-1907, The Eisinger, Kramer & Co. Catalogue 1899-1900. 174,175—Charles J. Van Schaick Collection, State Historical Society of Wisconsin. 176—Culver Pictures. 177—State Historical Society of Wisconsin. 178,179—The Byron Collection, Museum of the City of New York—Kansas State Historical Society, quote from *Ladies' Home Journal*, January 1910, © The Curtis Publishing Co. 181—Brown Brothers. 182—Sy Seidman. 183—Culver Pictures. 184—From *Life*, October 4, 1900—From *Life*, October 11, 1900. 185—From *Life*, October 18, 1900—From *Life*, November 8, 1900. 186,187—From *Life*, November 29, 1900. 188—From *Life*, December 6, 1900—From *Life*, December 20, 1900. 189—From *Life*, January 10, 1901—From *Life*, February 21, 1901. 190,191—From *Life*, April 25, 1901; From *Life*, June 27, 1901; From *Life*, July 4, 1901. 192,193,195—Culver Pictures. 196,197—McGreevey Collection, Boston Public Library. 198,199—Missouri Historical Society. 200—Underwood & Underwood. 201—Bettmann Archive. 202,203—From *Life*, August 15, 1902. 205—Brown Brothers. 206—Culver Pictures. 208,209—Morris Rosenfeld & Sons. 210—Brown Brothers. 211—From *Life*, June 5, 1902. 212—Culver Pictures. 213—Brown Brothers; Culver Pictures. 214—Culver Pictures. 215—Brown Brothers; United Press International. 216,217—Evelyn Hofer. 218,219—Lee Boltin. 221—Brown Brothers. 222,223—Morris Rosenfeld & Sons. 224,225—Brown Brothers. 226,227—Automotive History Collection, Detroit Public Library. 229—From *Life*, July 11, 1901. 230,231—Brown Brothers. 232,233—Automotive History Collection, Detroit Public Library. 234,235—Culver Pictures. 236—From *Handbook of Early American Advertising Art*, Dover Publications. 237—From *Life*, May 12, 1910 (Hank Ehlbeck). 238—From *Life*, August 15, 1907 (Hank Ehlbeck). 239—From *Life*, February 17, 1910 (Hank Ehlbeck); from *Life*, October 21, 1909 (Hank Ehlbeck)—From *Life*, May 6, 1909 (Hank Ehlbeck); from *Life*, April 14, 1910 (Hank Ehlbeck). 240—From *Life*, January 7, 1909, Sy Seidman. 241—Automobile Manufacturers Association. 242,243—Brown Brothers. 245—Sy Seidman. 246,247—Culver Pictures except top right (2) Brown Brothers. 248,249—Culver Pictures; cards by Sy Seidman. 251,252—Culver Pictures. 253—Brown Brothers. 254,255—Culver Pictures. 257—Brown Brothers. 258—Sy Seidman. 259—All Sy Seidman, except bottom left "School Days" by Will D. Cobb & Gus Edwards, © 1906 by Mills Music Inc. © Renewed 1934 by Mills Music Inc. (Culver Pictures); bottom right "My Wife's Gone to the Country, Hurrah, Hurrah!" by George Whiting, Irving Berlin and Ted Snyder.© 1909 Irving Berlin, © Renewed 1936 Irving Berlin, used by permission of Irving Berlin Music Corporation. 260—Circus World Museum, Baraboo, Wisconsin. 261—Culver Pictures. 262,263—Manchester Historical Society. 264,265—The Jackson Collection, Henry Ford Museum, Dearborn, Michigan (Joe Clark). 267—Brown Brothers. 268,269—Keystone View Co.; Frank Nowell Library, University of Washington, Seattle. 270,271—State Historical Society of Wisconsin. 272,273—The Jackson Collection, Henry Ford Museum, Dearborn, Michigan (Joe Clark). 274,275—Henry E. Huntington Library and Art Gallery; State Historical Society of Wisconsin. 276,277—State Historical Society of Wisconsin. 278 through 281—Minnesota Historical Society.

# Acknowledgments

*The editors of this book wish to thank the following persons and institutions for their assistance:*

Yeatman Anderson III, Public Library of Cincinnati and Hamilton County, Cincinnati, Ohio; Mrs. Lois Barland, Chippewa Valley Historical Society, Eau Claire, Wisconsin; Dr. John Blackburn, Hollywood, California; Mr. Boston Distiller, Inc., Roxbury, Massachusetts; Don Boyett, Managing Editor, *Amarillo Globe News*, Amarillo, Texas; James J. Bradley, Director, Automotive History Collection, Detroit Public Library; Beatrice Buda, Museum of the City of New York; Edwin H. Carpenter, Western Americana Bibliographer, Henry E. Huntington Library and Art Gallery, San Marino, California; Harry Collins, Brown Brothers, New York City; Mrs. Robert Crowe, Montebello, California; John Cumming, Director of Clarke Historical Library, Central Michigan University, Mt. Pleasant; Virginia Daiker, Prints and Photographs Division, Library of Congress; Mrs. Alice Dalligan, Curator of Manuscripts, Detroit Public Library; James Davis, Librarian, Western History Department, Denver Public Library; Mr. Richard A. Ehrlich, Boston; Mrs. Ruth K. Field, Curator of Pictures, Missouri Historical Society, St. Louis; Gibson House, Boston; The Gillette Company, Boston; Dorothy Gimmestad, Assistant Picture Curator, Minnesota Historical Society, St. Paul; Marshall Hail, *El Paso Herald-Post*, El Paso, Texas; Alison Kallman, New York City; Jack Krueger, Executive Editor, *Dallas Morning News;* Thomas K. Leinbach, Administrator, The Historical Society of Berks County, Reading, Pennsylvania; Mrs. Alice Roosevelt Longworth; Helen

MacLachlin, Curator, Theodore Roosevelt Birthplace, New York City; Mary Jane Maddox, *Marshall News Messenger*, Marshall, Texas; Mr. Elmo Mahoney, Dorrance, Kansas; Alexandra Mason, Director, Department of Special Collections and Mrs. Jane E. Riss, Curator, Regional History Division, University of Kansas Libraries, Lawrence; Robert D. Monroe, Chief of Special Collections Division, University of Washington Library, Seattle; Sol Novin, Culver Pictures, New York City; The Preservation Society of Newport County, Newport, Rhode Island; Mrs. Elizabeth Rademacher, Michigan Historical Commission Archives, Lansing; Stanley Rosenfeld, New York City; Janet Coe Sanborn, Curator, Cleveland Picture Collection, Ohio; Sy Seidman, New York City; Joseph W. Snell, Assistant State Archivist and F. R. Blackburn, Newspaper and Census Division, Kansas State Historical Society, Topeka; Claude Stanush, San Antonio, Texas; Gerald Talbot, Director, Museum Village of Smith's Clove, Monroe, New York; Mrs. Lawrence Tilley, Rhode Island Historical Society, Providence; John Barr Tompkins, Public Services Director, The Bancroft Library, University of California, Berkeley; Mrs. Judith Topaz, Assistant, Iconographic Collections, State Historical Society of Wisconsin, Madison; Gregory C. Wilson, Curator, Theodore Roosevelt Collection, Harvard College Library; Mrs. John A. Wipperfurth, Tomahawk, Wisconsin; Mrs. Geneva Kebler Wiskemann, Reference Archivist, Michigan Historical Commission Archives, Lansing.

# Bibliography

Allen, Frederick Lewis, *The Big Change*. Bantam Books, Inc., 1965.

Amory, Cleveland, *The Last Resorts*. Universal Library, Grosset & Dunlap, Inc., 1952.

Amory, Cleveland, *Who Killed Society?* Harper & Row Publishers, 1960.

Anderson, Rudolph E., *The Story of the American Automobile*. Public Affairs Press, 1950.

Atherton, Lewis, *Main Street on the Middle Border*. Quadrangle Books, Inc., 1966.

Balsan, Consuelo Vanderbilt, *The Glitter and the Gold*. Harper & Row Publishers, 1952.

Barrett, Richmond, *Good Old Summer Days*. D. Appleton-Century Co., 1941.

Blum, Daniel, *A Pictorial History of the Silent Screen*. Grosset & Dunlap, Inc., 1953.

Canby, Henry Seidel, *American Memoir*. Houghton Mifflin Co., 1947.

Cantor, Norman F., and Michael S. Werthman, eds., *The History of Popular Culture*. Macmillan Company, 1968.

Churchill, Allen, *The Great White Way*. E. P. Dutton & Co., Inc., 1962.

Cohn, David L., *Combustion on Wheels*. Houghton Mifflin Co., 1944.

Cohn, David L., *The Good Old Days*. Simon and Schuster, Inc., 1940.

Corsi, Edward, *In the Shadow of Liberty*. Macmillan Company, 1935.

Eliot, Elizabeth, *Heiresses and Coronets*. McDowell, Obolensky, 1959.

Ewen, David, *The Life and Death of Tin Pan Alley*. Funk & Wagnalls Co., 1964.

Faulkner, Harold U., *The Quest for Social Justice 1898-1914*. Macmillan Company, 1931.

Fox, Charles Philip, *A Ticket to the Circus*. Superior Publishing Co., 1959.

Freudenthal, Elsbeth, *Flight into History, The Wright Brothers and the Air Age*. University of Oklahoma Press, 1949.

Fulton, A. R., *Motion Pictures*. University of Oklahoma Press, 1960.

Hagedorn, Hermann, ed., *The Roosevelt Family of Sagamore Hill*. Macmillan Company, 1954.

Howe, Edgar Watson, *The Story of a Country Town*. Twayne Publishers, 1962.

Hughes, Glenn, *A History of the American Theatre, 1700-1950*. Samuel French, Inc., 1951

Johnston, William Davison, *T.R.: Champion of the Strenuous Life*. Farrar, Straus & Cudahy, 1958.

Langford, Gerald, *The Murder of Stanford White*. Bobbs-Merrill Co., Inc., 1962.

Laurie, Joe Jr., *Vaudeville*. Henry Holt & Co., 1953.

Lord, Walter, *The Good Years*. Bantam Books, Inc., 1965.

Mattfeld, Julius, *Variety Music Cavalcade, 1620-1961*. Prentice-Hall, Inc., 1962.

May, Earl Chapin, *The Circus from Rome to Ringling*. Dover Publications, Inc., 1963.

Mayer, Grace, *Once Upon a City*. Macmillan Company, 1958.

Morris, Lloyd, *Not So Long Ago*. Random House, Inc., 1949.

Morris, Lloyd, *Postscript to Yesterday*. Random House, Inc., 1947.

Roosevelt, Theodore, *An Autobiography*. Charles Scribner's Sons, 1946.

Smith, Cecil, *Musical Comedy in America*. Theatre Arts Book, 1950.

Spaeth, Sigmund, *A History of Popular Music in America*. Random House, Inc., 1948.

Steffens, Lincoln, *The Shame of the Cities*. Peter Smith, 1948.

Stern, Phillip Van Doren, *A Pictorial History of the Automobile*. Viking Press, Inc., 1953.

Wagenknecht, Edward, *The Seven Worlds of Theodore Roosevelt*. Longmans, Green & Co., 1958.

Wheeler, Thomas C., ed., *A Vanishing America: The Life and Times of the Small Town*. Holt, Rinehart & Winston, Inc., 1964.

White, William Allen, *Forty Years on Main Street*. Farrar & Rinehart, 1937.

Whitehouse, Arch, *The Early Birds*. Doubleday & Co., Inc., 1965.

*Year* editors, *Flight, A Pictorial History of Aviation*. Year, Inc., 1953.

# Index

*Numerals in italics indicate an illustration of the subject mentioned.*